C000067073

healthy
SLOW COOKER

SLOW COOKER

Over 60 recipes for nutritious, home-cooked
meals from your electric slow cooker

Nicola Graimes
with Cathy Seward

photography by Peter Cassidy

RYLAND PETERS & SMALL
LONDON • NEW YORK

Author and recipe developer Nicola Graimes
Technical consultant, recipe tester
and Americanizer Cathy Seward

Senior designer Sonya Nathoo
Editor Miriam Catley
Production manager Gordana Simakovic
Art director Leslie Harrington
Editorial director Julia Charles
Publisher Cindy Richards

Photographer Peter Cassidy
Food stylists Kathy Kordalis and Sian Henley
Prop stylist Luis Peral
Indexer Vanessa Bird

Originally published in 2017 as *Superfood Slow Cooker*.
This updated edition published in 2022
by Ryland Peters & Small
20–21 Jockey's Fields, London WC1R 4BW
and
341 E 116th St, New York NY 10029

www.rylandpeters.com

10 9 8 7 6 5 4 3 2 1

Notes

• All recipes are made in a 3.5-litre/6-pint slow cooker.
• All nutritional breakdowns relate to one serving
of the individual recipes and exclude all
accompaniments.
• Always completely defrost meat, poultry, seafood
and shellfish before adding to the slow cooker.
• Both British (Metric) and American (Imperial plus
US cups) measurements are included in these recipes
for your convenience, however it is important to work
with one set of measurements and not alternate
between the two within a recipe.
• All spoon measurements are level unless otherwise
specified.
• All eggs are medium (UK) or large (US), unless
specified as large, in which case US extra-large
should be used. Uncooked or partially cooked eggs
should not be served to the very old, frail, young
children, pregnant women or those with compromised
immune systems.
• Whenever butter is called for within these recipes,
unsalted butter should be used.
• When a recipe calls for the grated zest of citrus fruit,
buy unwaxed fruit and wash well before using. If you
can only find treated fruit, scrub well in warm soapy
water before using.

Disclaimer

The views expressed in this book are those of the
author but they are general views only and readers are
urged to consult a relevant and qualified specialist or
physician for individual advice before beginning any
dietary regimen. Ryland Peters & Small hereby exclude
all liability to the extent permitted by law for any errors
or omissions in this book and for any loss, damage or
expense (whether direct or indirect) suffered by a third
party relying on any information contained in this
book. You should always consult your physician before
changing your dietary regimen.

Contents

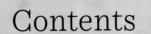

Introduction

Nurturing, restorative and nutritious, there's something really quite special about a slow-cooked meal. It's almost an antidote to hectic, modern life and the preoccupation with quick meals and fast food. The beauty of slow cooking is partly its simplicity and I've tried to maintain this with the recipes in this book using readily available, nutritious, fresh ingredients and cooking them in a simple, unfussy, economic way.

Healthy ingredients don't have to be exotic, expensive or only found in specialist shops. Simple, everyday fresh foods have the power to support and boost our health but for me, it's more than just about physical wellbeing – healthy ingredients can be as good for the soul as they are for the body. Just consider a tasty, nutritious bowl of filling soup made with a nurturing bone broth and lots of veg – it ticks all the right boxes.

When you think of slow cooking, rich, hearty stews, soups and curries immediately spring to mind – basically winter comfort food – but I was surprised to discover, as you may be, while creating these recipes that my slow cooker is so much more versatile than I'd given it credit for. Think parcels of lightly cooked fish, crisp balls of falafel, light, fluffy cornbread, melt-in-the-mouth 'baked' sweet potatoes and even crisp, golden granola.

Slow cookers cook food gently and evenly and it is arguable that the lower cooking temperature may actually help to preserve nutrients that can be lost when food is cooked quickly at high heat, such as frying, grilling/broiling and boiling. Additionally, since the food is contained within a covered pot, nutrients released from the food could be contained in the slow cooker within any liquid or sauce; although, fat-soluble vitamins (A, D, E and K) tend to hold up better than water-soluble ones such as vitamins B and C.

Cooking foods slowly at a lower temperature is also less likely to expose us to advanced glycation end products (AGEs), which are toxins created by grilling/broiling and frying foods at high temperatures, especially meat and other animal products. AGEs have been linked to Alzheimer's disease, inflammation, diabetes, vascular and kidney disease as well as ageing skin.

To enable you to eat good healthy food at any time of the day, the recipes in this book cover most eating occasions, from breakfast and brunch to weekday meals and dishes more suited to weekend cooking. With the Weekday Meals chapter, I've been mindful to include recipes that can be assembled in the morning, cook through the day and ready when you get home from work. Some dishes may require finishing just before serving, but pretty much all the hard work is done by the slow cooker.

The true beauty of a slow cooker is that dishes pretty much look after themselves – there's no need to hover over the hob/stove top to produce healthful, nutritious, tasty meals loaded with superfoods.

About the recipes

All the recipes in this book have been double tested in a 3.5-litre/6-pint/4-quart slow cooker and mainly feed four people. Only the high and low settings were used as these are standard on all models and the slow cooker was not preheated.

One of the slow cookers used for testing had a lightweight metal, non-stick coated pot that could be used on the hob/stove top for pre-browning and tended to cook more quickly than the second slow cooker with its heavier ceramic pot. Each recipe comes with range of cooking times – the shorter time tells you that the food will be tender and ready to eat but will not deteriorate if left to cook for the longer time given. It also allows for differences in performance between the many models of slow cooker available.

Choosing a slow cooker

Slow cookers come in many variations with features and prices to suit all needs. If you are thinking of buying a slow cooker there are a few things to consider.

What size?
Generally speaking slow cookers are available in three basic sizes – small, medium and large and may be oval or round in shape. The working capacity is always less than stated on the packaging as you must not fill the slow cooker right to the brim.

Round or oval?
Round slow cookers are a good choice if you are going to cook mainly soups and stew type recipes. An oval pot is a little more versatile and is an ideal shape for cooking joints of meat and whole chickens.

Features
Removable inner pots These are made from stoneware, ceramic or lightweight non-stick coated metal. Stoneware and ceramic pots are heavier to lift and cannot be used on the hob/stove top but look great taken to the table for serving. Metal pots can be used directly on the hob/stove top for pre-browning and searing foods – the pot is then placed in the base unit – so much quicker and more convenient. These pots are lighter to lift, too, so it's easier to pour and serve or turn out foods. Metal pots may cook a little faster than those made from stoneware and ceramic so cooking times may be shorter in these models. Always check the manufacturer's instructions.

Transparent lids A clear toughened glass or heavy-duty plastic lid will allow you to keep an eye on the food as it's cooking.

Digital controls Some models have digital controls that enable you to set the cooking time on the unit. It will count down and automatically switch to 'keep warm'. This is useful if you don't want to use a separate timer.

Settings
Slow cookers reach just below boiling point 100°C/212°F during cooking – this temperature is reached more quickly on the high setting. All models vary slightly in performance – some cook more quickly than others. You will soon get used to your own model.

Basic cookers just have low and high settings and an 'off' position. Some may also have a medium, auto or warm setting.
Low for long, slow, all-day, or overnight cooking – great for putting a meal in the pot before you go out for the day or go to bed.
High if you want to speed up the cooking time – generally takes half the time of the low setting.

You can use a combination of low and high if you want to add thickeners to a recipe at the end of the cooking time or add foods such as seafood – simply switch to high for the time specified in your recipe.

Auto available on some models – this setting automatically switches the cooker from high to low after about 1 hour and enables you to reach the optimum temperature more quickly and reduce the cooking time slightly. If your model does not include this setting you can start the recipe on the high setting for 1 hour and then switch to the low setting manually, adjusting the cooking time accordingly.

Warm At the end of the cooking time this setting can be used to keep the food at the correct serving temperature. Never use this setting for cooking.

USING THE SLOW COOKER
Always follow the manufacturer's instructions supplied with your cooker because the actual method of use can vary from model to model.

Some manufacturers recommend preheating the cooker on the high setting 20–30 minutes before adding the food. Others say to heat the pot only when you are about to add the food.

The recipes in this book have not included a preheating instruction. If your instruction manual states that this must be carried out it is important that you do so.

Capacities
Make sure your cooker is at least half full when cooking meat, fish and vegetable dishes. Joints of meat should take up no more than two-thirds of the space. Always leave some headroom and never fill the pot right to the top.

Pre-browning
Pre-browning ingredients, especially meat, enhances the appearance of the food and can improve the flavour but it isn't essential. However, minced/ground beef, lamb or pork should be pre-browned for best results as it stops it clumping together. Pre-browning can be done in a separate frying pan/skillet or alternatively, directly in the pot if it can be used on the hob/stove top.

Lifting the lid
Don't be tempted to lift the lid and stir the food. Food won't stick and burn or boil over in the slow cooker.It is important to remember that every time you lift the lid you will have to add 20 minutes to the cooking time to compensate for the drop in temperature. Only lift the lid if stated in the recipe and make sure it is replaced promptly.

COOKING TIMES
All the recipes in this book include a range of cooking times. This means that the food will be cooked and ready to eat at the lower time but it can be left without spoiling for the maximum time given. Always cook for the minimum time given in the recipe but adjust times according to your own particular model. Some cook faster and some cook slower – especially if you have an older slow cooker.

The cooking times can also be affected by conditions in your kitchen. If the kitchen is very hot you may find that the cooking times are shorter. If it's a very cold day the food may need longer cooking. Similarly, if the slow cooking pot has been refrigerated, let it come to room temperature before cooking. Slow cooking is not an exact science so there are variables that can affect the cooking performance and this should always be taken into account.

Cooking times will vary but approximate comparative cooking times on low and high are as follows:

Low setting	High setting
4–8 hours	1½–4 hours
8–10 hours	5–6 hours
10–12 hours	7–8 hours

Slow cooker size guide:

SIZE	MAX CAPACITY	SERVINGS
Small	1.5 litres/2½ pints/ 1.5 quarts	1–2 servings Ideal for couples or 1 to 2 person households
Medium	3.5 litres/6 pints/4 quarts	3–4 servings (depending on the recipe) – ideal for small families
Large	6.5 litres /11½ pints/ 6 quarts	6–8 servings Great for larger quantities and batch cooking

Healthy foods for the slow cooker

MEAT

A complete protein and rich in essential fats, vitamins, including many Bs and D, and minerals such as zinc and iron, red meat offers many nutritional benefits and can play a part in a balanced, varied diet. While red meat isn't essential in our diets, it's worth remembering around two-thirds of us are believed to be deficient in iron. Red meat is a particularly good source of the mineral and in a more readily absorbable form than that found in vegetables or other plant foods.

If you eat meat, always go for the best quality you can afford and that means lean, organic, grass-fed and free-range – and opt for a few meatless days each week, swapping it for plant-based proteins such as beans and pulses.

The recipes featuring red meat in this book do so in small, yet nutritious, quantities and you'll find it is supplemented with lots of fresh vegetables or other plant foods. Slow cooking helps to extract a pure meaty flavour that permeates the whole dish, so it is possible to use smaller amounts. Slow cookers are perfect for making nutritious bone broths using beef, pork or lamb bones (see page 16).

Preparation/cooking tips

• Choose inexpensive cuts of meat for slow cooking such as brisket, stewing/chuck steak, silverside/ top round/bottom round/eye of round, lamb shoulder, neck fillet, pork shoulder/Boston butt.
• Make sure joints are even in size so they cook evenly. Try not to select a joint that tapers as the thin end will cook more quickly than the thick part, causing the joint to overcook in places.
• Trim away excess fat and cut into even bite-size pieces – or according to the recipe.
• Pre-brown or bring to room temperature before adding to the slow cooker.
• It's a good idea to check the internal temperature of cooked food, especially joints of meat and whole chicken, with a food thermometer. Insert the probe into the thickest part – food should reach an internal temperature of 75°C/165°F.

POULTRY

Chicken contains a similar amount of protein to red meat, but with less fat and fewer of the unhealthy bits attributed to red meat. A complete protein, chicken provides all the essential amino acids necessary for the growth, repair and maintenance of the body. It's particularly rich in B vitamins, especially B6 and B3 (niacin); the former supports the immune system, metabolism and the central nervous system, while B3 is responsible for maintaining the health of the body's cells and converting carbohydrates to energy.

The antioxidant selenium is also found in beneficial amounts and is thought to protect against many major illnesses, including cancer and heart disease, as well as inflammatory diseases.

Slow cookers are perfect for cooking chicken broths, soups and stews with their restorative and immune-boosting properties – there is some truth in the old wives' tale! Studies show that these chicken dishes could provide relief from upper respiratory cold symptoms and if you throw in plenty of veg, ginger, turmeric and garlic, you further increase their health benefits and immune-boosting properties.

Buy organic and free-range chicken if possible, which has been found to have a greater concentration of nutrients, particularly increased levels of omega-3 fatty acids.

Preparation/cooking tips

• Whole chicken cooks beautifully in the slow cooker. Marinate in flavoursome ingredients to add colour or pre-brown before cooking.
• Chicken thighs are a good choice – they remain moist and delicious.
• Remove the skin from chicken portions, if preferred.

FISH & SHELLFISH

While cooking seafood in a slow cooker may sound an anomaly, it can be perfect as it cooks it gently and evenly. One of the easiest and most nutritious methods is to wrap the fish in a baking paper or foil parcel, which keeps the flavours, juices and nutrients contained and works well with more fragile fish that has a tendency to fall apart. Add vegetables, spices and herbs to the fish parcels and you further lift the nutritional value.

The perfect superfood, fish is an excellent low-fat source of protein, vitamins and minerals if eaten regularly – two portions are recommended a week, one of which should be oily. A single portion of oily fish, such as salmon, mackerel, trout, sardines, pilchards or tuna, per week is said to benefit the health and condition of the heart, brain, joints, skin and eyes due to the omega-3 fatty acid content. It is also one of the few food sources of vitamin D, a nutrient many of us are lacking.

Being slightly firmer in texture, salmon, tuna and mackerel cook beautifully in a slow cooker and needn't be wrapped in a parcel. They are ideal cooked on top of a thick vegetable-based or bean stew and ideally should be added towards the end of the cooking time to retain their nutrients, texture and flavour. Shellfish, such as mussels, clams and crab, also provide beneficial amounts of omega-3 fatty acids, along with the minerals copper, zinc, magnesium and iron as well as protein.

Preparation/cooking tips
Fish
• Ideal for all types of fish, whole, pieces or fillets.
• Fish can be wrapped in foil parcels and layered in the pot or can be cooked unwrapped in or on top of a sauce.
• Cooking times tend to be short so add towards the end of the cooking time according to the recipe – cook until the flesh is opaque and flaky.

Shellfish
• Always add towards the end of the cooking time to avoid overcooking and toughening.
• Add to the cooker on the high setting.
• Pat dry to remove excess liquid.

VEGETABLES

Vegetables are the ultimate superfood and ideally should play a major part of every meal. To benefit from the widest range of nutrients, phytochemicals and antioxidants go for variety and colour.

There is patchy, if any, respected research on nutrient loss from food that is cooked for long periods, but nutritionally some vegetables respond better to being cooked than eaten raw. For instance, cooking enhances the antioxidant content of tomatoes; while combining them with a fat, such as olive oil, increases the body's ability to absorb nutrients found in the fruit.

Slow cooking is a gentle way to cook and since temperatures are kept below boiling point (see page 8), it is arguable that more nutrients are preserved than when vegetables are cooked rapidly at a high heat, such as when boiled, grilled/broiled or fried. Additionally, since the vegetables are contained within a covered pot, any nutrients released are contained in the slow cooker within any liquid, stock or sauce.

The beauty of cooking in a slow cooker is that most vegetables don't need to be peeled and since many nutrients are found in, or just below, the skin this is no bad thing (the skin also provides valuable fibre).

Make use of sea vegetables in your slow cooking, too. For instance, nori, wakame and kombu are incredibly rich in minerals such as iodine, zinc, calcium, magnesium, manganese, potassium and trace elements including selenium. Dried nori or wakame can be sprinkled over dishes, while kombu added to a cooking pot of dried beans will help soften them and curb any unwanted side effects.

Cooking/preparation tips

• Some vegetables – especially root vegetables such as carrots, beetroot/beets, turnips and parsnips can take longer to cook than meat in most cookers so cut into small even-sized dice/slices/bite-sized pieces according to the recipe and place under the meat or poultry. However, the latter is not always the case in modern slow cookers and may not be necessary. You may find that the vegetables softened very well without placing them at the bottom of the pot, so could just be tipped into the pot with the other ingredients.

• Add delicate vegetables such as broccoli, asparagus and leafy greens towards the end of the cooking time to avoid overcooking and loss of colour and nutrients. Baby spinach and chopped kale can just be added at the end and stirred through the mixture – they will cook in the heat of the food.

• Cut potatoes tend to discolour if not submerged in the cooking liquid so push them down into the pot.

PULSES/DRIED BEANS

Beans and pulses respond beautifully to slow cooking. In the main, the recipes cook these humble ingredients in their dried soaked form (see below for tips), but you can use canned if easier or where suggested. Cheap to buy and brimming with nutrients, beans and pulses provide a range of vitamins, minerals and fibre, including folic acid, magnesium, iron, potassium and B vitamins. They are also rich in both complex carbohydates and protein so should be one of your go-to ingredients for good health. (Both the American Heart Association and American Cancer Society recommend beans and pulses as one of the most important food groups for disease prevention.)

Dried beans and pulses should be soaked (see right), since not only does this speed up the cooking time, it helps improve their digestibility. If put off by their gaseous after-effects, add a strip of dried kombu seaweed to the cooking pot – ginger, fennel or cumin can help, too, as well as boosting the nutrient content of the dish. Alongside their health benefits, pulses add extra substance to your cooking.

Preparation/cooking tips

• Pulses and dried beans contain a toxin that must be removed before cooking. The following method MUST be carried out before they can be cooked in the slow cooker. It is advisable to carry out this method of preparation for all varieties when cooking in the slow cooker even if the pack instructions say that this is not necessary. Pulses and dried beans MUST be soaked overnight in plenty of cold water to soften them. After soaking, drain them and put into a pan with fresh water. Bring to the boil, then boil rapidly for 10 minutes. We recommend boiling for an additional 10 minutes to tenderize them at this stage, then drain the beans and add to the slow cooker.

• The only exceptions to this rule are red, green and Puy lentils. These do not need to be soaked and boiled before adding to the slow cooker.

• Do not add salt to pulses and dried beans until the end of the cooking time as it toughens them.

FRUIT

Most of the recipes in this book are savoury, with the exception of a few breakfast dishes. That said, fresh and dried fruits are added to some of the savoury stews and curries to enhance their flavour, texture and nutritional value. When possible, avoid peeling fresh fruit to retain its fibre content as well as nutrients found in, or just below, the skin.

Although dried fruit is super-sweet, it is a good source of iron, magnesium, potassium and calcium. Similarly, the fibre content is higher than in fresh.

Preparation/cooking tips

• Dried and fresh fruit cooks well, retaining colour, texture and flavour.

RICE & GRAINS

Easy cook/quick cook rice (see below) works best in a slow cooker with the grains retaining their shape and texture. The good news is that there is no appreciable difference in nutrient profile between brown easy-cook/quick cooking and regular wholegrain rice.

Opt for brown wholegrain rice instead of refined white – it's a much better source of fibre, vitamins and minerals, including magnesium, selenium and manganese, and is surprisingly high in antioxidants. Additionally, it is a low glycaemic food, which means that it helps keep blood-sugar levels stable.

Other wholegrains such as barley, faro, spelt, kamut and jumbo oats also hold their own when slow cooked without turning mushy. They provide a catalogue of beneficial nutrients as well as fibre, which aids digestive health, improving nutrient absorption, immunity and promoting good bacteria in the gut.

Preparation/cooking tips

• Always use easy-cook/quick cooking rice. Ordinary rice tends to become very mushy.
• Use coarser jumbo oats for porridge to give a good consistency rather than quick cook or fine cut oats.
• Always eat cooked rice as soon as it is cooked and do not leave it sitting at room temperature – cooked rice contains spores that can cause food poisoning if not handled correctly. If you are not eating rice or a rice dish immediately, remove from the pot at the end of the cooking time, cool as quickly as possible (ideally within 1 hour) and store in the fridge.
• Don't leave cooked rice on the 'keep warm' setting for food safety reasons and also to avoid overcooking.

FATS

Slow cooking can be a low-fat method of food preparation. When cooking soups and stews, for instance, it's perfectly feasible to bung the main ingredients into the pot without adding any oil or fat. That said, the right fats provide numerous health benefits and are essential for the body to function normally – some vitamins need the presence of fat to be absorbed by the body.

Recently, there's been a review in thinking by health experts relating to fats and health, with studies showing that saturated fat may be better for us than previously thought. It appears that there is now insufficient evidence to support the theory that saturated fat increases the risk of heart disease.

Coconut oil and ghee (clarified butter) are used in the recipes for curries and Asian-style dishes. Both are stable oils when heated and offer a range of health benefits, too. Coconut oil has a strong, distinctive flavour that suits Asian dishes and is rich in medium-chain fatty acids. It is said to be antiviral, antifungal and antibacterial as well as helping to increase levels of good cholesterol in the body. This promotes good health heart and helps improve brain and memory function. Look for extra-virgin unrefined coconut oil, which is purer and the best quality.

Ghee is a very stable fat and is rich in fat-soluble vitamins and minerals, including the antioxidant selenium. Find it in pots in the Asian section in supermarkets or in Asian grocers.

Olive oil is also used in the book and as a monounsaturated fat it is rich in antioxidants and is good for the health of the heart and cognitive function.

Other types of beneficial fats in the book include avocado, butter, oily fish (omega-3 fatty acids) and cold-pressed rapeseed oil, which is a world away from regular highly processed rapeseed oil.

Preparation/cooking tips

• Cooking meat over a long period can release a lot of fat, so trim away any excess fat before cooking.
• Remove any excess oil from the surface at the end of cooking using paper towels or a skimmer.

HERBS, SPICES & SALT

Herbs and spices not only lift and enhance the flavour and interest of a dish, they benefit our health, too. Herbs such as basil, coriander/cilantro, bay, dill, mint, oregano and thyme, are all said to aid digestion and have a carminative effect on the stomach, easing indigestion and nausea. Similarly, many spices are renowned for their digestive properties.

Additionally, spices help to reduce the need for salt in cooking as they significantly enhance the flavour of food. They also feature a wide range of antioxidants and are believed to increase metabolism, particularly chilli/chile, which has been found to aid weight loss.

Turmeric could be hailed as the spice of the moment but it has been revered in the Far East for many hundreds of years, particularly as an anti-inflammatory. Numerous studies also suggest it has antioxidant, antiviral and antibacterial properties. Curcumin is the active ingredient and is more bioavailable if consumed with piperine, a compound in black pepper. Buy turmeric as a fresh root or in dried powdered form – organic is best as it is non-irradiated.

Ginger is excellent for digestion and gastro problems, particularly nausea. An anti-inflammatory, it has been found to reduce the symptoms of, and pain associated with, arthritis.

Sea salt is used throughout the book, rather than highly processed table salt. Rich in trace minerals, it promotes balanced acid/alkaline levels in the body and restores electrolyte balance. Do be mindful of the amount you consume.

Preparation/cooking tips

• Fresh herbs can easily become overcooked losing their flavour so add them at the end.
• Dried herbs are more robust so can be added at the beginning of the cooking process.
• Spices can also lose some of their flavour during slow cooking so add more according to your taste to compensate for this.

• Some dishes can taste saltier so reduce the amount of salt added to a recipe.

LIQUIDS

Many of the recipes in this book feature stock, whether vegetable, chicken, fish or meat. You can use ready-made but on page 16 you'll also find a selection of nutritious homemade stocks and broths, all of which are cheap to prepare, make use of leftovers and waste, and come without unwanted additives. The bone broths are abundant in nutrients, are probiotic and rich in both collagen and keratin. Excellent for good health, they also improve the condition of the skin, hair and nails.

Cooking/preparation tips

• To ensure the correct temperatures are reached safely it is important to use hot stock or water in most cases. This helps to give a boost in temperature at the start of the cooking process.
• There is very little evaporation from a slow cooker so less liquid may be needed. If you find there is too much liquid at the end of the cooking time simply remove the lid and cook on high for approx. 30 minutes until the liquid has reduced.

THICKENERS

Kuzu, a root that has been used in Japanese cooking for thousands of years, is a superior gluten-free thickener and comes with many health properties. Usually sold in large granules, kuzu is renowned for its digestive and calming qualities and is good for treating indigestion and cold symptoms.

Preparation/cooking tips

• It is best to thicken a recipe at the end of the cooking.
• Use cornflour/cornstarch or kuzu blended with a little cold water, stir into the pot, turn the setting to high and cook covered or uncovered for 15–20 minutes or until thickened.
• If the pot can be used on the hob/stove top add thickeners and bring to the boil, stirring.
• Alternatively, pour/decant into a separate saucepan, add thickeners and bring to the boil, stirring until thickened.

Rich vegetable stock

If mushrooms aren't your thing, do swap them for parsnip, tomatoes, leeks and/or fennel. To intensify the flavour of the stock, you could roast the onions, carrots and celery first.

1 tablespoon olive oil
2 onions, thinly sliced
3 carrots, sliced
2 celery sticks, sliced
175 g/6 oz. mushrooms, sliced
1 large handful parsley stalks

½ teaspoon peppercorns
2 bay leaves
sea salt

Low 6–7 hours
High 4–5 hours

Makes about 1.5 litres/6 cups

Heat the oil in a large frying pan/skillet, add the onions and fry for 8 minutes until softened. Add the carrots, celery and mushrooms and cook for another 5 minutes. Tip the onion mixture into the slow cooking pot. Add the remaining ingredients and 1.5 litres/6 cups just-boiled water. Cover and cook on low for 6–7 hours, or on high for 4–5 hours, until the vegetables are very tender.

Strain the stock through a sieve/strainer, discarding the bay leaves. Press the solids through the sieve/strainer with the back of a spoon.

Skim and season the stock with salt. To concentrate the flavour of the stock return it to the slow cooker and cook it on high, uncovered, until reduced. Alternatively, you can do this in a saucepan on the hob/stove top. Store in the fridge for up to 3 days or 3 months in the freezer.

Chicken Broth Variation: Don't waste the chicken carcass left over from a roast. Put it in the slow cooker pot with the flavourings listed for the 12-Hour Bone Broth (right), and cover with just-boiled water. Cover and cook on low for 6–10 hours. Follow the instructions for straining, draining and cooling (right). Return it to the slow cooker or pour into a saucepan and cook uncovered until reduced. Store in the fridge for up to 3 days or 3 months in the freezer.

12-hour bone broth

A labour of love, but you'll be blessed for your patience with a nourishing, nutrient-laden, probiotic, collagen- and keratin-rich, stomach-soothing, flavoursome beef broth.

1.5 kg/3 lb. 5 oz. beef bones
1 onion, cut into wedges
1 carrot, thickly sliced
1 celery stick, thickly sliced
2 bay leaves

10 peppercorns

Low 12–16 hours (or longer if you like)

Makes about 1 litre/4 cups

Put the bones in a large saucepan, cover with cold water and bring to the boil over a high heat. Turn the heat down slightly and cook for 25 minutes before draining.

Preheat the oven to 240°C (475°F) Gas 9. Spread out the bones on two baking sheets then roast for 30–40 minutes until browned and caramelized.

Tip the bones into the slow cooker pot and add the remaining ingredients. Pour in enough just-boiled water from a kettle to cover the bones – about 1.7 litres/7 cups. Cover and cook on low for 12 hours, or longer if time allows. At 12 hours the broth will have reduced slightly, so if you intend to cook it for longer, top it up with some more just-boiled water from the kettle, about 200 ml/¾–1 cup. Cover and continue to cook for another 4 hours or longer, if you like.

Using tongs, lift out and discard the bones then strain the broth, pressing the vegetables through the sieve/strainer. Store in the fridge for up to 3 days or 3 months in the freezer.

Breakfast
and Brunch

Apple spice porridge

There's something quite decadent about waking up to a pot of comforting, sustaining porridge – all ready to be spooned into serving bowls. To stop the porridge drying out, it's best cooked in a bain marie/water bath set within the slow cooker; it also makes washing up easier. If cooked on low it's feasible to let it cook overnight without spoiling, but if you prefer your porridge with a bit of bite and texture, cook it on high for a shorter length of time – it will still be lovely and creamy.

125 g/1½ cups jumbo porridge oats
1 teaspoon good-quality vanilla extract
1 heaped teaspoon mixed spice/apple pie spice, plus extra for sprinkling
½ teaspoon turmeric
pinch of sea salt
2 apples, cored and grated
ground flaxseeds/linseeds, chopped walnuts, blueberries and milk, of choice, to serve

Low 7–8 hours
High 2½–3 hours

Serves 3–4

Mix together the oats, vanilla, mixed spice/apple pie spice, turmeric, salt and 700 ml/3 cups cold water in a 1 litre/1 quart heatproof bowl until combined. Place the bowl in the slow cooker pot and pour in enough cold water to come two-thirds of the way up the side of the bowl if cooking on low. (If cooking on high for the shorter length of time, add hot water.)

Cover and cook on low for 7–8 hours, or high for 2½–3 hours, until thick and creamy. Towards the end of the cooking time, stir in one of the grated apples and let it soften in the heat of the porridge – it will take about 10 minutes.

Using oven gloves/mitts, carefully lift out the bowl and stir well to remove any crusty bits around the edge, if necessary. Spoon the porridge into serving bowls and top with the remaining grated apple, flaxseeds/linseeds, walnuts and blueberries as well as a sprinkling of extra mixed spiced/apple pie spice. You may like to add a splash of milk as well.

NUTRITIONAL INFORMATION
223 kcals, 3.9 g fat (0.6 g saturates), 38.4 g carbohydrate, 11.6 g sugars), 4.4 g fibre, 5.2 g protein, 0.1 g salt

Raw cacao and coconut porridge

Rich in antioxidants and said to elevate mood, raw cacao is made by cold-pressing unroasted cacao beans and so retains a lot of the nutrients reduced or lost in more processed forms of chocolate or cocoa. To conserve these qualities, stir the raw cacao powder into the porridge towards the end of the cooking time. The porridge is made with coconut drinking milk, but you could use half water or, indeed, all water, if you prefer.

125 g/1½ cups jumbo porridge oats
700 ml/3 cups coconut drinking milk from a carton, plus extra for serving, and/or water
1 teaspoon good-quality vanilla extract
1 heaped teaspoon ground cinnamon, plus extra for sprinkling
6 pitted dates, finely chopped
pinch of sea salt
1 tablespoon raw cacao powder
diced mango, toasted flaked coconut and chopped pecans, to serve

Low 7–8 hours
High 2½–3 hours

Serves 3–4

Mix together the oats, coconut drinking milk and/or cold water, vanilla, cinnamon, dates and salt in a 1 litre/1 quart heatproof bowl until combined.

Place the bowl in the slow cooker pot and pour in enough cold water to come two-thirds of the way up the side of the bowl if cooking on low. (If cooking on high for the shorter length of time, add hot water.)

Cover and cook on low for 7–8 hours, or high for 2½–3 hours, until thick and creamy. Just before serving, mix the cacao powder with a little extra coconut milk to make a smooth, creamy paste and stir it into the porridge.

Using oven gloves/mitts, carefully lift out the bowl and stir well to remove any crusty bits around the edge, if necessary. Spoon the porridge into serving bowls and top with the mango, flaked coconut and pecans, as well as a sprinkling of extra cinnamon. You may like to add an extra splash of coconut milk, too.

NUTRITIONAL INFORMATION
269 kcals, 6.6 g fat (3.3 g saturates), 44 g carbohydrate (14.1 g sugars), 5.5 g fibre, 6.2 g protein, 0.4 g salt

Chai-spiced fruit compote

Inspired by masala chai – an Indian spiced black tea – this dried fruit compote is enhanced with a blend of restorative, reviving spices and rooibos tea. It's cooked slowly overnight until rich, sticky and almost caramelized, and a spoonful is all you need to liven up a bowl of thick live plain yogurt.

450 g/1 lb. mixed dried fruit, such as figs, prunes/dried plums, unsulphured apricots, apple rings
juice of 2 oranges
finely grated zest of 1 orange
1 small cinnamon stick
3 cloves
3 cardamom pods, split
4-cm/1½-in. piece root ginger, sliced into rounds
1 rooibos tea bag
thick live plain yogurt and nuts and seeds, to serve

Low 7–8 hours
High 4–5 hours

Serves 12

Put the dried fruit, orange juice, orange zest and spices in the slow cooker pot. Pour in 300 ml/1¼ cups cold water and stir until combined.

Cover and cook on low for 7–8 hours, or 4–5 hours on high, adding the rooibos tea bag 30 minutes before the end of the cooking time. The fruit compote will be soft, sticky and thick, but do add extra water (hot if you want to serve it warm), if you prefer more 'juice'.

Just before serving, pick out and discard the rooibos tea bag, cinnamon stick, cardamom pods, cloves and ginger. Serve warm or cold on top of yogurt with a sprinkling of nuts and seeds.

To turn the compote into a rich fruit jam, blend until smooth then stir in 1 tablespoon chia seeds and leave for 30 minutes to thicken.

NUTRITIONAL INFORMATION
111 kcals, 0.2 g fat (0 g saturates), 25.9 g carbohydrate (25.8 g sugars), 0.9 g fibre, 1 g protein, trace salt

Maple pecan granola

This isn't the most obvious recipe to include in a slow cooker book, but amazingly it works, is nutrient-dense and flavourwise is more than a match for the overly sweet, shop-bought alternatives. I like to use quinoa flakes as they up the protein count, but if you can't find them increase the quantity of jumbo oats instead.

175 g/2 cups jumbo porridge oats
100 g/1 cup quinoa flakes
50 g/⅓ cup sesame seeds
50 g/heaping ⅓ cup sunflower seeds
150 g/1 cup pecan nut halves, roughly chopped
1 tablespoon ground cinnamon
6 tablespoons coconut oil
100 ml/⅓ cup good-quality maple syrup
1 teaspoon good-quality vanilla extract
3 tablespoons shelled hemp seeds
2 tablespoons chia seeds
85 g/3 oz. pitted dates, chopped
dried and/or fresh fruit, live plain yogurt or milk and ground flaxseeds/ linseeds, to serve

Low 2½–3 hours

Makes about 650 g/ 1 lb. 7 oz.

Mix together the porridge oats, quinoa flakes, seeds, pecans and ground cinnamon in the slow cooker pot.

Put the coconut oil, maple syrup and vanilla in a small saucepan and heat gently, stirring, until the oil has melted. Pour the mixture into the pot and stir well until combined and everything is evenly coated.

Cover the top of the slow cooker with paper towels and put on the lid to secure the paper in place (the paper will help to absorb any steam in the pot). Cook on low for 2½–3 hours until slightly golden and crisp (the granola will crisp up further when left to cool). Stir the granola twice during the cooking time, taking care not to leave the lid off the pot for too long to avoid losing too much heat. Keep an eye on the granola towards the end of the cooking time to avoid it burning or catching on the base.

Tip the granola onto 2–3 parchment paper-lined baking sheets, spread it out evenly and leave to cool and crisp up. When cold, stir in the shelled hemp seeds, chia seeds and dates and tip, using the parchment paper to help you, into a large storage jar. The granola will keep for up to 2 weeks.

Serve the granola in bowls topped with fruit, yogurt or milk, and ground flaxseeds/linseeds.

NUTRITIONAL INFORMATION
205 kcals, 13.4 g fat (4.2 g saturates), 16.2 g carbohydrate (6.3 g sugars), 2.6 g fibre, 4 g protein, trace salt

Best baked beans

This simple breakfast-cum-brunch encapsulates what slow cooking is all about…
it's nutritious, easy and economical. Dried beans do need a little forward
planning – pre-soak for 6–8 hours, or overnight, and they must be boiled for
10 minutes before adding to the slow cooker. I also recommend simmering for
another 10 minutes to make sure they soften enough – there's nothing worse
than tough beans. No worries if you forget to pre-prepare the beans, canned
haricot/navy beans are a good alternative and mean you can reduce the cooking
time by a couple of hours on either high or low.

**250 g/1¼ cups dried
haricot/navy beans,
soaked overnight**
1 onion, grated
**400 g/14 oz. can chopped
tomatoes**
**1 tablespoon blackstrap
molasses**
**1 tablespoon tomato
purée/paste**
**1 tablespoon smoked
paprika**
**1 heaped teaspoon Dijon
mustard**
1 teaspoon ground ginger
**1 teaspoon apple cider
vinegar**
**sea salt and cracked black
pepper**

Low 7–8 hours
High 5–6 hours

Serves 4

Drain and rinse the soaked beans and tip them into a large
saucepan. Cover with plenty of cold water and bring to the boil.
Let the beans boil rapidly for 10 minutes, then turn the heat down
and simmer for another 10 minutes. Drain the beans, discarding
the cooking water, and tip them into the slow cooker pot.

Add the rest of the ingredients to the pot, apart from the
seasoning (salt toughens uncooked beans), then pour in
500 ml/2 cups hot water. Cover and cook on low for 7–8 hours,
or high for 5–6 hours, until the beans are tender.

Season, to taste, with salt and pepper and serve the baked beans
in your own favourite way – in a bowl with a fried egg on top
is delicious!

NUTRITIONAL INFORMATION
238 kcals, 1.6 g fat (0.3 g saturates), 41 g carbohydrate (11.5 g
sugars), 4 g fibre, 15.8 g protein, 0.4 g salt

Chilli/chile cornbread with avocado and black bean salsa

100 g/7 tablespoons butter, ghee or coconut oil, melted, plus extra for greasing
200 g/1 cup coarse polenta
100 g/²⁄₃ cup spelt flour
2 teaspoons baking powder
½ teaspoon bicarbonate of soda/baking soda
¾ teaspoon sea salt
1 teaspoon English mustard powder
2 tablespoons ground flaxseeds/linseeds
1 medium-sized red chilli/ chile, deseeded and diced
3 eggs, lightly beaten
300 ml/1¼ cups live plain yogurt
juice of ½ lemon

AVOCADO AND BLACK BEAN SALSA
1 large avocado, peeled, stoned/pitted and diced
juice of ½–1 lime
100 g/²⁄₃ cup canned black beans, drained and rinsed
3 vine-ripened tomatoes, deseeded and diced
1 small red onion, diced
½ red (bell) pepper, deseeded and diced
1 medium-sized red chilli/ chile, deseeded and diced
1 tablespoon extra virgin olive oil
sea salt and cracked black pepper

High 2–3 hours

Makes 1 loaf

The cornbread is given a nutrient boost with the addition of ground flaxseeds/linseeds, which are one of the few vegetarian sources of omega-3 fatty acids.

Line the base of the slow cooker pot with baking parchment. Roll two long pieces of parchment paper into 2.5 cm/1 in. wide strips to form two handles. Place the strips under the base lining and up the sides so they hang over the top of the pot. Liberally grease the sides of the pot.

Mix together all the dry ingredients and chilli/chile in a mixing bowl, then make a well in the centre.

Whisk together the melted butter, ghee or coconut oil, eggs, yogurt and lemon juice until smooth. Pour into the dry ingredients and mix gently and thoroughly to make a thick batter.

Pour the batter into the slow cooker pot and smooth and level the top. Cover and cook on high for 2 hours – the cornbread is ready when a skewer inserted into the centre comes out clean and the edge is slightly golden. If it isn't quite ready, cover and cook on low for another 30 minutes–1 hour and check again. When ready, leave the cornbread to sit in the slow cooker for 5 minutes with the lid off then transfer to a wire rack.

To make the avocado and black bean salsa, toss the avocado in the juice of ½ lime to stop it discolouring. Put all the remaining ingredients in a bowl, add the lime-dressed avocado and season with salt and pepper. Turn gently until combined and taste, adding more lime juice if needed. Cut the cornbread into slices and serve with the avocado and black bean salsa.

NUTRITIONAL INFORMATION
1/10th of a loaf 244 kcals, 12.6 g fat (6.5 g saturates), 23.3 g carbohydrate (3.3 g sugars), 3.1 g fibre, 6.1 g protein, 1.1 g salt

Sweet potato hash

More weekend brunch than weekday breakfast...
the idea is to make this sweet potato version of the
classic hash first thing and then go back to bed while it
cooks! The Brussels sprouts and cauliflower are added
towards the end so they give a slight crunch in contrast
to the soft sweet potato and also retain their precious
nutrients. A poached egg and a sprinkling of fresh
coriander/cilantro and chopped chilli/chile add the
finishing touches.

1 tablespoon ghee or
    coconut oil
1 large onion, finely
    chopped
2.5-cm/1-in. piece
    root ginger,
    coarsely grated
100 g/3½ oz. red
    cabbage, shredded
2 teaspoons panch
    phoran
2 sweet potatoes,
    about 200 g/7 oz.
    each, cut into
    small bite-sized
    pieces
300 ml/1¼ cups hot
    vegetable stock
150 g/5½ oz.
    Brussels sprouts,
    thinly sliced

2 large cauliflower
    florets, coarsely
    grated
sea salt and cracked
    black pepper
poached eggs,
    coriander/cilantro
    leaves and diced
    red chilli/chile, to
    serve

High 3–4 hours

Serves 4

Heat the ghee or coconut oil in a large frying
pan/skillet and sauté the onion for 8 minutes
until softened. Stir in the ginger, red cabbage,
panch phoran and sweet potatoes and cook for
another minute.

Tip the sweet potato mixture into the slow cooker
pot and pour in the stock. Cover and cook
on high for 2½ hours. Stir in the sprouts,
returning the lid promptly, and cook for another
30 minutes–1 hour by which time the sweet
potato should be lovely and tender and almost
starting to break down. Season and stir in the
grated cauliflower – there is no need to cook it
as the cauliflower will soften in the residual heat.

Season with salt and pepper and spoon the
hash into shallow serving bowls. Serve topped
with a poached egg and a sprinkling of
coriander/cilantro and chilli/chile.

NUTRITIONAL INFORMATION
188 kcals, 4.2 g fat (2.9 g saturates), 28.3 g
carbohydrate (13.3 g sugars), 6.9 g fibre, 4.6 g
protein, 0.7 g salt

Smoky roasted red (bell) pepper tortilla with chermoula

This tortilla is surprisingly easy to cook in a slow cooker. The texture is marginally different to one that is pan-cooked but is still delicious, especially served with the chermoula – a surefire way to add extra oomph to the morning. Eggs have impressive health credentials; as a complete protein they provide all eight essential amino acids as well as valuable amounts of vitamins and minerals.

butter, for greasing
8 eggs
300 g/10½ oz. cooked new potatoes in their skins, cubed
150 g/5½ oz. roasted red (bell) peppers from a jar, drained, patted dry and roughly chopped
sea salt and cracked black pepper
grilled/broiled tomatoes, to serve

CHERMOULA
1 large handful chopped basil leaves
1 large handful chopped flat-leaf parsley
1 small garlic clove, finely chopped
1 medium-sized green chilli/chile, deseeded and finely chopped
juice of 1 lemon
2 tablespoons extra virgin olive oil
sea salt

Low 2–3 hours

Serves 4

To make the chermoula, mix together all the ingredients in a bowl and season with salt. Serve at room temperature.

Line the base of the slow cooker pot with parchment paper. To make the tortilla easier to lift out, roll two long pieces of parchment paper into 2.5 cm/1 in. wide strips to form two handles. Place the strips under the base lining and up the sides so they hang over the top of the pot. If you have a light slow cooker pot, this step may not be necessary as the tortilla can simply be turned out onto a plate. Grease the sides of the pot with butter.

Crack the eggs into a mixing bowl and lightly beat with a fork. Stir in the cooked potatoes and roasted red (bell) peppers and season with salt and pepper, then pour the mixture into the slow cooker pot. Cover and cook on low for 2–3 hours until just set and slightly golden around the edges.

Lift or turn out the tortilla and cut it into wedges. Serve warm or cold with the chermoula and grilled/broiled tomatoes.

NUTRITIONAL INFORMATION
226 kcals, 11.5 g fat (3.6 g saturates), 13.5 g carbohydrate (4 g sugars), 2 g fibre, 16 g protein, 0.6 g salt

Kitchiri

A filling, sustaining bowl of goodness. This spiced Indian breakfast is a nutritionally balanced combination of brown rice and lentils, while the soft-boiled/soft-cooked egg adds a protein boost as well as folate and vitamins A, B12 and D. While brown basmati would normally be my rice of choice, easy-cook/quick cooking brown rice works best in a slow cooker, retaining its texture and separate grains, without turning into a homogenous mass.

1 tablespoon ghee or coconut oil
1 large onion, finely chopped
2.5-cm/1-in. piece root ginger, grated
2 garlic cloves, finely chopped
3 cardamom pods, seeds ground
1 teaspoon turmeric
1 tablespoon garam masala
200 g/1 cup easy-cook/quick cooking brown rice
100 g/½ cup (drained weight) canned green lentils
300 ml/1¼ cups almond milk
4 soft-boiled/soft-cooked eggs
1 medium-sized green chilli/chile, deseeded and finely chopped (optional)
1 tablespoon nori flakes
sea salt and cracked black pepper

APPLE RAITA
100 ml/½ cup live plain yogurt or dairy-free alternative
1 red-skinned apple, grated and core discarded
juice of ½–1 lime
1 handful of chopped mint leaves
sea salt

Low 3–4 hours
High 2–3 hours

Serves 4

Heat the ghee or coconut oil in a large frying pan/skillet, add the onion and fry for 8 minutes until softened. Stir in the ginger, garlic, spices and rice and cook for another minute.

Tip the onion mixture into the slow cooker pot and stir in the lentils, almond milk and 300 ml/1¼ cups water. Season with salt and pepper. Cover and cook on low for 3–4 hours, or high for 2–3 hours, until the liquid is absorbed and the rice is tender. Turn off the slow cooker and let the rice sit for 5 minutes.

To make the apple raita, mix together all the ingredients in a bowl and season with salt.

Serve the rice in bowls, topped with a halved soft-boiled/soft-cooked egg, chilli/chile, if using, nori flakes and a spoonful of apple raita.

NUTRITIONAL INFORMATION
334 kcals, 10.7 g fat (4.4 g saturates),
45 g carbohydrate (4.5 g sugars), 4.5 g fibre,
14.5 g protein, 0.5 g salt

Light Bites

Lemony mung bean hummus

Don't be put off by the worthy sounding name – mung beans make a surprisingly creamy hummus and without the graininess of those made with chickpeas/garbanzo beans. Additionally, they are a good source of fibre, protein and minerals. Due to the lower cooking temperature of the slow cooker, I tend to boil the mung beans for 10 minutes beforehand. Crisp baked wholewheat pitta breads, brushed with olive oil and sprinkled with sesame seeds are perfect for dunking.

100 g/½ cup dried mung beans, rinsed and soaked for a minimum of 4 hours or overnight

3 tablespoons light tahini

1 large garlic clove, crushed

juice of 1 lemon

1 tablespoon extra virgin olive oil, plus extra for drizzling

sea salt and cracked black pepper

diced red (bell) pepper, chilli/red pepper flakes and chopped parsley, to serve

Low 5–6 hours
High 4–5 hours

Serves 6

Drain and rinse the mung beans and tip them into a saucepan. Cover with plenty of cold water and bring to the boil, then boil rapidly for 10 minutes. Let the beans boil rapidly for 10 minutes, then drain the beans, discarding the cooking water, and tip them into the slow cooker pot.

Cover with just-boiled water from a kettle. Cover and cook on low for 5–6 hours, or high for 4–5 hours until tender.

Drain the mung beans thoroughly and tip them into a food processor. Add the tahini, garlic, lemon juice and olive oil and blend until light, smooth and creamy. You may need to add a little extra lemon juice or water and stir the hummus occasionally to help everything on its way.

Season with salt and pepper and spoon the hummus into a serving bowl. Top with the diced red (bell) pepper, chilli/red pepper flakes and parsley then drizzle with extra olive oil before serving. The hummus will keep stored in an airtight container in the fridge for up to 3 days.

NUTRITIONAL INFORMATION
135 kcals, 8.9 g fat (1.3 g saturates), 7.3 g carbohydrate (0.4 g sugars), 1.7 g fibre, 6.1 g protein, 0.1 g salt

Smoky sweet potato hummus

Make sure you buy orange-fleshed sweet potatoes, not only do they add to the visual appeal of this hummus but they are much richer in beta carotene than the white-fleshed alternative. It is important to include oil in sweet potato-based dishes as it helps to increase the uptake of the beta carotene, which is converted to vitamin A in the body.

3 sweet potatoes, about 250 g/9 oz. each
1 tablespoon hot smoked paprika
125 ml/½ cup Greek live yogurt
4 tablespoons light tahini
juice of 1 lemon
1 large garlic clove, crushed
2 teaspoons pomegranate molasses
1 tablespoon extra virgin olive oil
1 tablespoon toasted sesame seeds
1 small handful chopped coriander/cilantro
sea salt and cracked black pepper

Low 6–7 hours
High 4–5 hours

Serves 6–8

Scrub the sweet potatoes, pat dry, and place them in the slow cooker pot. Cover and cook on low for 6–7 hours, or high for 4–5 hours, until the sweet potatoes are tender when pierced with a skewer. Remove from the slow cooker and leave to cool.

Cut the cooled potatoes in half and scoop the flesh into a large bowl. Add the paprika, yogurt, tahini, lemon juice, garlic and half the pomegranate molasses, then mash with a potato masher to a hummus-like consistency. You could also blend it in a food processor, if you prefer a smoother end result. Season with salt and pepper and spoon the hummus into a serving bowl.

Drizzle the remaining pomegranate molasses over the top of the hummus with the olive oil then sprinkle over the sesame seeds and coriander/cilantro. The hummus can be stored in an airtight container in the fridge for up to 3 days.

NUTRITIONAL INFORMATION
259 kcals, 12.9 g fat (3 g saturates), 28.3 g carbohydrate (9.9 g sugars), 4.3 g fibre, 5.4 g protein, 0.3 g salt

Warm summer salad

This warm Mediterranean-style salad captures the flavours of summer and is an excellent way of using up a glut of vegetables. Tomatoes left to ripen on the vine have a greater nutritional value and higher lycopene content than those picked too early, so it's well worth looking out for them. This recipe is similar to a vegetable confit, but uses less olive oil, and will keep in the fridge for up to 3 days – do bring it back to room temperature before serving for the best flavour. I don't brown the onion beforehand, this is one recipe where is doesn't seem to make a difference to the final taste and texture of the dish.

1 teaspoon vegetable bouillon powder

3–4 tablespoons extra virgin olive oil

a pinch of saffron threads, soaked in a little warm water, or ½ teaspoon turmeric

12 baby carrots, cut in half lengthways

150 g/5½ oz. runner/string beans, thinly sliced diagonally

1 large red onion, thinly sliced

4 good-size, vine-ripened tomatoes, cut in half and then into thin wedges

2 courgettes/zucchini, cut into 1 cm/½ in. thick half moons

2 garlic cloves, thinly sliced

1 small unwaxed lemon, cut in half

3 large basil sprigs

sea salt and cracked black pepper

Low 4–5 hours
High 3–4 hours

Serves 4

Dissolve the vegetable bouillon powder in 3 tablespoons hot water.

Put all the ingredients, including the vine from the tomatoes (if you have it), in a slow cooker pot. Cover and cook on low for 4–5 hours, or high for 3–4 hours, until the vegetables are tender.

Remove the basil, tomato vine, if using, and lemon halves and serve warm or at room temperature. Season with salt and pepper.

NUTRITIONAL INFORMATION
233 kcals, 14.1 g fat (2.2 g saturates), 18 g carbohydrate (15.2 g sugars), 6.9 g fibre, 4.6 g protein, 0.9 g salt

Beetroot/beet soup with apple and hazelnut

This rich, velvety, vibrant soup comes with a topping of Greek yogurt, diced apple and toasted hazelnuts, which not only add flavour and contrast in texture, but also boost the nutritional value. When it comes to nutrients, beetroot/beets are valued for their blood pressure-lowering nitrate content alongside iron, folate and magnesium.

1 tablespoon olive oil

1 large onion, finely chopped

2 carrots, finely chopped

1 stick celery, finely chopped

2 garlic cloves, finely chopped

750 g/1 lb. 10 oz. raw beetroot/beets, cut into very small dice

2 green apples

850 ml/3½ cups hot vegetable stock, plus extra if needed

2 teaspoons cumin seeds

1 teaspoon caraway seeds

squeeze of lemon juice

4 tablespoons live Greek yogurt

1 handful toasted hazelnuts, roughly chopped

sea salt and cracked black pepper

Low 6–7 hours
High 5–6 hours

Serves 4–6

Put the olive oil, onion, carrots, celery, garlic and beetroot/beets into the slow cooker pot. Grate one of the apples into the pot, discarding the core, then pour in the hot stock. Cover and cook on low for 6–7 hours, or high for 5–6 hours, until the vegetables are tender. You can cook the soup for a couple of extra hours without spoiling the flavour or texture.

Meanwhile, toast the cumin and caraway seeds in a dry, non-stick frying pan/skillet for a minute until they smell aromatic, then tip into a bowl and set aside until ready to serve.

Blend the soup using a stick blender until smooth, adding a little more stock if needed – the soup should be silky smooth and fairly thick. Season with salt and pepper.

Dice the remaining apple, discarding the core, and toss it in the lemon juice to stop it discolouring. Ladle the soup into bowls and top with a swirl of yogurt, the toasted spices, diced apple and toasted hazelnuts.

NUTRITIONAL INFORMATION
219 kcals, 7.7 g fat (2 g saturates), 28.1 g carbohydrate (24.6 g sugars), 7.3 g fibre, 6.2 g protein, 1.4 g salt

Super pea soup

Visually, fresh green vegetables do not respond well to slow cooking, losing their colour and turning a bit murky looking. Nutritionally, this is also probably the case. Rather than lose out on the impressive health benefits of green vegetables, the peas, spring onions/scallions and spinach are added at the last minute and are cooked just long enough to soften but still retain their colour and nutritional value. For a lower fat version, leave out the ghee or coconut oil.

150 g/¾ cup dried split peas, soaked overnight

1 tablespoon ghee or coconut oil

1 large onion, finely chopped

1 large carrot, diced

1 celery stick, thinly sliced

2 bay leaves

1 litre/4 cups hot vegetable stock

350 g/3 cups frozen peas, defrosted and drained

5 spring onions/scallions, thinly sliced

2 handfuls chopped mint leaves

50 g/2 cups baby spinach leaves, finely chopped

sea salt and cracked black pepper

55 g/2 oz. feta cheese, crumbled, and toasted pumpkin seeds, to serve

Low 8–9 hours, plus 20 minutes on high
High 7½–8½ hours

Serves 4

Drain and rinse the soaked peas and tip them into a large saucepan. Cover with plenty of cold water and bring to the boil. Let the beans boil rapidly for 10 minutes, skimming any froth that rises to the surface, then turn the heat down and simmer for another 10 minutes. Drain the peas, discarding the cooking water, and tip them into the slow cooker pot.

Add the ghee or coconut oil, onion, carrot, celery, bay leaves and vegetable stock to the pot. Stir well until combined then cover and cook on low for 8–9 hours, or high for 7–8 hours, until the split peas are tender.

Turn the slow cooker to high, if cooking on low. Add the defrosted peas, spring onions/scallions and half the mint. Cover and cook for 20 minutes, then season and stir in the spinach – there's no need to cook it as the finely chopped leaves will soften in the heat of the soup.

Using a stick blender or a food processor, blend the soup until smooth and thick. Check the seasoning, adding more salt and pepper, if needed, but taking into account the feta is quite salty. Ladle the soup into serving bowls and top with crumbled feta, pumpkin seeds and the remaining chopped mint.

NUTRITIONAL INFORMATION
292 kcals, 5.1 g fat (2.9 g saturates), 41 g carbohydrate (15 g sugars), 11.6 g fibre, 15.2 g protein, 1.9 g salt

White bean, leek and cashew soup

The cashews not only add a rich, buttery, creaminess to this vegan soup, they are also an excellent source of vitamins and minerals. They also provide high levels of the antioxidant lutein, which has been shown to protect the eyes from light damage. As an added bonus, the nutritional yeast flakes add valuable B vitamins.

1 tablespoon olive oil
3 leeks, thinly sliced
1 large onion, thinly sliced
2 celery sticks, thinly sliced
3 garlic cloves, chopped
400 g/14 oz. can butter-
    beans/lima beans,
    drained
1 teaspoon dried thyme
1 bay leaf
1 litre/4 cups hot vegetable
    stock
Cashew Cream (see page 55)
100 g/1⅓ cups cauliflower
    florets, grated
3 tablespoons nutritional
    yeast flakes
sea salt and cracked black
    pepper
2 tablespoons snipped
    chives, to serve

GREMOLATA
2 handfuls chopped parsley
1 small garlic clove,
    crushed
finely grated zest
    of 1 unwaxed lemon
2 teaspoons lemon juice
splash of extra virgin olive
    oil

Low 5–6 hours, plus 15
minutes on high
High 3¼–4¼ hours

Serves 4

Put the olive oil, leeks, onion, celery, garlic, butterbeans/lima beans, thyme, bay leaf and hot stock in the slow cooker pot. Cover and cook on low for 5–6 hours, or high for 3–4 hours, until the leeks are tender.

While the soup is cooking, make the cashew cream following the instructions on page 55. To make the gremolata mix together all the ingredients in a bowl and season with a little salt.

Remove the bay leaf and, using a stick blender, blend the soup until smooth. Stir in the cashew cream, cauliflower florets and nutritional yeast flakes and season with salt and pepper. Turn the slow cooker to high if on low, and warm through for 10–15 minutes.

Serve the soup topped with a spoonful of gremolata and a sprinkling of chives.

NUTRITIONAL INFORMATION
324 kcals, 14.1 g fat (2.9 g saturates), 27.4 g carbohydrate (14.6 g sugars) 11.9 g fibre, 16.2 g protein 2 g salt

Asian broth with crab

Cleansing, reviving and restorative for the digestive system, this fragrant lemongrass, kaffir lime, chilli/chile and ginger broth has added sweet potato 'noodles' and fresh crab to make it more substantial. Brown rice noodles or soba noodles are also good, but cook them separately and add to the serving bowl before spooning over the broth. You could make the Asian broth up to a day ahead to let it infuse for longer – just strain and reheat it before resuming the recipe from *.

1 litre/4 cups hot fish stock
4 kaffir lime leaves
5-cm/2-in. piece root ginger, sliced
2 garlic cloves, thinly sliced
2 onions, thinly sliced
2 long lemongrass stalks, bruised
2 teaspoons fish sauce
1 medium-sized red chilli/chile, cut in half lengthways and deseeded
15 g/⅛ cup goji berries (optional)
550 g/1lb 4 oz. sweet potato, peeled and spiralized, or cut into fine strips

6 spring onions/scallions, thinly sliced diagonally
2 large handfuls kale, leaves finely chopped
juice of ½ lime, plus 1 lime, cut into wedges
300 g/10½ oz. crabmeat
1 handful chopped coriander/cilantro
2 teaspoons nori flakes (optional)
sea salt and cracked black pepper

Low 3–4 hours, plus 45 minutes on high
High 2¾–3¾ hours

Serves 4

Pour the hot stock into the slow cooker pot and add the lime leaves, ginger, garlic, onions, lemongrass, fish sauce and half the red chilli/chile. Cover and cook on low for 3–4 hours, or high for 2–3 hours, to let the flavourings infuse the stock.

Using a slotted spoon or skimmer, spoon the solids into a bowl and discard leaving the broth in the pot.

*Turn the slow cooker to high if on low. Add the goji berries, if using, and sweet potato 'noodles', cover and cook for 45 minutes, adding the white parts of the spring onions/scallions and the kale 20 minutes before the end of the cooking time. The sweet potato 'noodles' are ready when just tender but still retain a little bite. Add a good squeeze of lime juice and season with salt and pepper.

Ladle the broth into four large shallow bowls. Spoon the crabmeat on top and sprinkle with the green parts of the spring onions/scallions, coriander/cilantro and nori flakes, if using. Dice the remaining red chilli/chile and scatter over before serving with extra wedges of lime for squeezing over.

NUTRITIONAL INFORMATION
259 kcals, 2.9 g fat (0.5 g saturates), 42 g carbohydrate (18.3 g sugars), 8 g fibre, 12.8 g protein, 2.9 g salt

Spiced carrot and lentil soup with cashew cream

Revered for centuries for their health-giving properties, spices play a big part in my cooking. One of my most favourite blends is panch phoran, a Bengali spice mix that literally means 'five spices'. The fragrant combination of fennel seeds, cumin seeds, fenugreek, black mustard seeds and nigella/charnushka seeds adds a great base note to this nutritious golden soup. It comes topped with a cashew cream, but is equally good with a spoonful of thick live natural yogurt.

1 tablespoon ghee or coconut oil

1 large onion, finely chopped

4 large carrots, about 600 g/1 lb. 5 oz., diced

1 large celery stick, thinly sliced

2 teaspoons panch phoran

5-cm/2-in. piece root ginger, coarsely grated

2 large garlic cloves, thinly sliced

140 g/heaped ⅔ cup dried split red lentils, rinsed

4 cardamom pods, bruised

½ teaspoon dried chilli/red pepper flakes

1 teaspoon ground turmeric

1 litre/4 cups hot vegetable stock

1 tablespoon lemon juice

sea salt and cracked black pepper

broccoli sprouts, to serve

CASHEW CREAM

70 g/½ cup cashew nuts

5 tablespoons milk of choice, plus extra if needed

Low 6–8 hours
High 4–5 hours

Serves 4

Heat the ghee or coconut oil in a saucepan, add the onion and sauté for 8 minutes until softened. Add the carrots, celery, panch phoran, ginger and garlic and sauté, stirring occasionally for another 2 minutes.

Transfer the onion mixture to the slow cooker pot, stir in the lentils, cardamom, chilli/red pepper flakes, turmeric and stock. Cover and cook on low for 6–8 hours, or high for 4–5 hours, until the lentils and carrots are tender.

Meanwhile, make the cashew cream. Put the cashew nuts in a bowl, cover with just-boiled water and leave to soak for 1 hour until softened. Drain the nuts and tip them into a food processor or blender with the milk of your choice. Blend, occasionally scraping the mixture down the sides, until a thick, creamy consistency – add a splash more milk, if needed. Spoon the cream into a bowl and chill until ready to serve.

Remove the cardamom pods from the soup – very conveniently they rise to the surface – and using a stick blender, blend until thick and smooth. Stir in the lemon juice and season with salt and pepper. Serve topped with a spoonful of the cashew cream and a few broccoli sprouts.

NUTRITIONAL INFORMATION
253 kcals, 4.5 g fat (2.8 g saturates), 37.9 g carbohydrate (16.6 g sugars), 9.6 g fibre, 10.7 g protein, 1.9 g salt

Slow-cooked aubergines/eggplant with courgette/zucchini tzatziki

Aubergines/eggplant respond beautifully to long, low cooking becoming meltingly soft and tender. Here, they are combined with the superfood trio of ginger, garlic and turmeric with their antibacterial, antiviral and antifungal properties. You could serve the aubergines/eggplant as a side dish, part of a meze with the tzatziki or as a main with the grain or your choice.

2 tablespoons ghee or coconut oil
500 g/1 lb 2 oz. aubergine/eggplant, cut into small pieces
1 onion, grated
2.5-cm/1-in. piece root ginger, grated
3 garlic cloves, grated
1 teaspoon turmeric
1 teaspoon nigella/charnushka seeds
2 teaspoons coriander seeds, ground
½ teaspoon dried chilli/red pepper flakes
1 tablespoon tomato purée/paste
1 teaspoon raw honey
sea salt and cracked black pepper
warm wholewheat chapattis, to serve

COURGETTE/ZUCCHINI TZATZIKI

100 ml/½ cup live plain yogurt
1 courgette/zucchini, coarsely grated
1 small garlic clove, grated
1 handful chopped mint
juice of 1 small lemon
sea salt and cracked black pepper

Low 6–7 hours
High 5–6 hours

Serves 4

Heat the ghee or coconut oil in a large frying pan/skillet, add the aubergine/eggplant and fry for 10 minutes until light golden – it will look as though there's not enough oil at first, but persist and the aubergine/eggplant will start to release the oil as it cooks. Stir in the onion, ginger, garlic and spices and cook, stirring, for another minute.

Tip the aubergine/eggplant mixture into the slow cooker pot and stir in the tomato purée/paste, honey and 250 ml/1 cup hot water. Cover and cook on low for 6–7 hours, or high for 5–6 hours, until the aubergine/eggplant is tender and the sauce is rich and thick – add a splash more hot water, if you feel it's needed. Season with salt and pepper.

To make the courgette/zucchini tzatziki, mix together all the ingredients in a bowl and season with salt and pepper.

Serve the aubergine/eggplant in bowls topped with a spoonful of the courgette/zucchini tzatziki and with the chapattis for dunking.

NUTRITIONAL INFORMATION
118 kcals, 7 g fat (5.4 g saturates), 8.6 g carbohydrate (7.2 g sugars), 4.8 g fibre, 2.3 g protein, 0.2 g salt

Beetroot/beet falafel with lemon tahini sauce

Low in fat and a good source of fibre, vitamins and minerals, these falafel have a surprisingly good crisp crust, while the centre remains lovely and moist.

100 g/½ cup dried
   chickpeas/garbanzo
   beans, soaked overnight
175 g/6 oz. cooked
   beetroot/beets, not in
   vinegar, patted dry, and
   quartered
2 garlic cloves, crushed
1 teaspoon ground cumin
1 teaspoon ground
   coriander
½ teaspoon dried chilli/
   red pepper flakes
2 tablespoons wholegrain
   spelt flour
4 tablespoons toasted
   sesame seeds
parsley, lemon wedges and
   wholewheat pitta bread,
   to serve

LEMON TAHINI SAUCE
150 ml/⅔ cup live plain
   yogurt
3 tablespoons light tahini
1 garlic clove, crushed
juice of ½ lemon
sea salt and cracked black
   pepper

High 3½–4 hours

Serves 4–6

Drain and rinse the soaked chickpeas/garbanzo beans and tip them into a large saucepan. Cover with plenty of cold water and bring to the boil. Let the chickpeas/garbanzo beans boil rapidly for 10 minutes, then turn the heat down and simmer for another 15 minutes until softened slightly but not cooked through. Drain the chickpeas/garbanzo beans and leave to cool.

Put the semi-cooked chickpeas/garbanzo beans in a food processor and blitz to coarse crumbs. Add the beetroot/beets, garlic and spices and blitz again until the mixture forms a coarse paste. Stir in the flour and seasoning. The mixture should look like a coarse, slightly wet paste and hold together when pressed into a ball.

Put the sesame seeds in a small bowl. Take a large marble-sized blob of the mixture and form it into a ball in the palm of your hand, then roll it in the sesame seeds until coated. Place the falafel on a plate and continue until you have about 30 in total. Chill for 30 minutes to firm up slightly. Line the slow cooking pot with greaseproof/waxed paper and arrange half of the falafel on top, spaced slightly apart. Place a second sheet of paper on top and arrange a second layer of falafel. Rest a paper towel to absorb any steam over the top of the slow cooker, then cover with the lid. Cook on high for 3½–4 hours until the falafel have an outer crust but are still moist inside. The bottom layer of falafel will cook slightly quicker than those on the top. If the second layer is too soft, return them to the slow cooker for another 20–30 minutes or until a crust forms on the outside.

NUTRITIONAL INFORMATION
313 kcals, 8.2 g fat (1.3 g saturates), 22.5 g carbohydrate
(5 g sugars), 5.9 g fibre, 10 g protein, 0.3g salt

Caponata with prawns/shrimp

Perfect served warm with crusty bread for mopping up the rich, tomatoey sauce. I tend to skip salting the aubergine/eggplant before cooking, unless it's particularly seedy, but it definitely benefits from sautéing before being added to the slow cooker, which ensures it's meltingly soft and adds both colour and flavour to the final dish. Avoid peeling the aubergine/eggplant as the skin provides valuable antioxidants and fibre.

2 tablespoons olive oil

1 aubergine/eggplant, cut into 1-cm/½-in. cubes

1 large onion, finely chopped

2 garlic cloves, finely chopped

1 tablespoon capers, drained and patted dry

600 g/3 cups canned chopped tomatoes

2 teaspoons dried oregano

1 medium-sized red chilli/chile, deseeded and diced

100 g/3½ oz. pitted kalamata olives

1 teaspoon red wine vinegar

250 g/9 oz. raw king prawns/jumbo shrimp, patted dry

sea salt and cracked black pepper

Low 5–6 hours
High 3–4 hours

Serves 4

Heat the oil in a large frying pan/skillet, add the aubergine/eggplant and fry for 5 minutes until starting to soften. Stir in the onion and cook for another 8 minutes until soft and starting to turn golden. Stir in the garlic and capers, cook for another minute then transfer to the slow cooker pot.

Stir in the chopped tomatoes, oregano, chilli/chile, olives and 100 ml/⅓ cup water. Cover and cook on low for 5–6 hours, or high for 3–4 hours, until the aubergine/eggplant is very tender.

40 minutes before the end of the cooking time, turn the slow cooker to high if on low. Add the red wine vinegar and prawns/shrimp and season with salt and pepper. Return the lid and cook until the prawns/shrimp are pink and cooked through.

NUTRITIONAL INFORMATION
237 kcals, 12.5 g fat (1.7 g saturates), 13.6 g carbohydrate (1⅓ g sugars), 4.9 g fibre, 14.6 g protein, 2 g salt

Hot soused herrings

Rich in brain-and heart-benefiting omega-3 fats, herrings are also a great source of vitamin D a deficiency of which could be a factor in many conditions, from diabetes and asthma to rickets, and is crucial in supporting the immune system. The wakame salsa provides a healthy boost. You can find dried wakame in large supermarkets and Asian grocers – it has a mild seaweed flavour and is rich in minerals, such as magnesium, iron, calcium and iodine.

175 ml/¾ cup apple cider vinegar

2 teaspoons raw honey

1 large pinch dried chilli/red pepper flakes

2 teaspoons coriander seeds

1-cm/½-in. piece root ginger, sliced into rounds

1 large red onion, very thinly sliced

2 cooked beetroot/beets, not in vinegar, thinly sliced (optional)

4 small herrings, gutted, cleaned and filleted

2 bay leaves

sea salt and cracked black pepper

WAKAME SALSA

15 g/½ oz. dried wakame seaweed

8-cm/3½-in. piece cucumber, diced

10 radishes, thinly sliced

¾ small red onion, diced

High 1¼–1½ hours

Serves 4

Put the vinegar, honey, chilli/red pepper flakes, coriander seeds and ginger in a small, non-metallic pan and bring to a gentle boil. Turn the heat down and simmer for 5 minutes. Leave for the flavours to infuse and cool, about 1 hour.

Place the sliced red onion and beetroot/beets in the base of the slow cooker pot. Rinse and pat the herring fillets dry and arrange them on top of the onions – it's fine if they slightly overlap.

Strain the vinegar mixture through a sieve/strainer into a jug/pitcher, discard the solids, and stir in 500 ml/2 cups just-boiled water from a kettle. Season with salt and pepper, stir, and pour the liquid over the fish. Add the bay leaves. Cover and cook on high for 1¼–1½ hours until the fish is opaque and flaky.

Meanwhile, make the wakame salsa. Put the wakame in a bowl and pour over enough cold water to cover. Leave for 5 minutes to soften, drain and tip into a bowl. Stir in the cucumber, radishes and onion and season with salt and pepper.

To serve, using a spatula, carefully lift out the herrings onto serving plates. Spoon over some of the cooking liquid. Serve with the wakame salsa on the side. The herrings and their cooking liquid can be left to cool and served cold.

NUTRITIONAL INFORMATION
244 kcals, 13.3 g fat (3.7 g saturates), 11 g carbohydrate (9 g sugars), 1.3 g fibre, 19.2 g protein, 0.5 g salt

Turkish Puy lentils with goat's cheese

Lentils just work in a slow cooker – it's a method of cooking that suits them perfectly, allowing them to soften low 'n' slow. Don't add the stock until towards the end of the cooking time as the salt toughens the lentils, as it does all dried pulses. Many large stores and Italian delis stock porcini stock cubes, but if you have difficulty finding them vegetable stock or bouillon powder is equally good. For their size, lentils are nutritionally impressive, providing plenty of cholesterol-lowering fibre along with valuable minerals, such as iron, zinc, potassium and copper, folate and many B vitamins.

1 tablespoon coriander seeds
2 tablespoons olive oil, plus extra for drizzling
1 large onion, finely chopped
4 carrots, quartered lengthways and cut into small bite-sized pieces
3 garlic cloves, finely chopped
1 medium-sized red chilli/chile, deseeded and diced
125 g/⅔ cup Puy lentils, rinsed
2 tablespoons tomato purée/paste
1 teaspoon brown rice syrup or raw honey
1 porcini stock cube, or vegetable alternative
squeeze of lemon juice
1 large handful chopped parsley
100 g/3½ oz. rindless goat's cheese, crumbled, or smoked tofu, cubed
sea salt and cracked black pepper

Low 7–8 hours
High 4–5 hours

Serves 4

Grind the coriander seeds in a pestle and mortar then set aside. Heat the oil in a large frying pan/skillet, add the onion and fry for 8 minutes until softened. Add the carrots, garlic, ground coriander seeds and chilli/chile, then cook for another minute.

Tip the onion mixture into the slow cooker pot and stir in the lentils, tomato purée/paste, brown rice syrup or honey and 400 ml/1½ cups hot water. Cover and cook on low for 7–8 hours, or high for 4–5 hours, until the lentils are tender but still hold their shape.

Stir in the stock or bouillon powder and add to the pot with a good squeeze of lemon juice as well as a splash more water, if needed – the lentils shouldn't appear too dry. Season with salt and pepper.

Spoon the lentil mixture onto serving plates, drizzle with extra olive oil and scatter over the parsley and goat's cheese or smoked tofu.

NUTRITIONAL INFORMATION
349 kcals, 16.2 g fat (5.9 g saturates),
31.2 g carbohydrate (13.2 g sugars),
7.7 g fibre, 15.1 g protein, 1.3 g salt

Sweet potatoes with salmon and pineapple and kale salsa

Baked sweet potato in a slow cooker? I know. I had to think twice about this recipe, bearing in mind that they are quicker to bake in the oven. That said, slow cookers compared to an oven cost a fraction to run and you could also leave the potatoes to do their thing with no intervention while you get on with your day. The sweet potatoes are topped with flakes of salmon and a pineapple salsa to give them a superfood boost.

4 sweet potatoes, about
   225 g/8 oz. each
2 cooked wild salmon
   fillets, skin removed and
   flaked

**PINEAPPLE AND KALE
SALSA**
225 g/8 oz. fresh pineapple
   chunks
½ small red onion, diced
4 heaped tablespoons
   chopped mint
1 handful curly kale, finely
   chopped
juice of 1 lime
½ medium-sized red
   chilli/chile, deseeded
   and diced (optional)
sea salt and cracked black
   pepper

Low 6–7 hours
High 4–5 hours

Serves 4

Scrub the potatoes, pat dry, and arrange them in the slow cooker pot – they can be placed on top of one another if they don't fit in a single layer. You can also wrap the potatoes in foil, which results in a slightly drier skin.

Rest a paper towel on top of the slow cooker to absorb any rising steam, then cover with the lid. Cook on low for 6–7 hours, or high for 4–5 hours, until tender when pierced with a skewer. (You could cook the sweet potatoes for an hour or so longer without detriment, if more convenient.)

While the potatoes are cooking, mix together all the ingredients for the pineapple and kale salsa and season with salt and pepper.

To serve, cut a cross into the top of the potatoes and press them open. Top with the pineapple and kale salsa and scatter over the flaked cooked salmon.

NUTRITIONAL INFORMATION
380 kcals, 8.1 g fat (1.7 g saturates), 53 g carbohydrate
(19.4 g sugars), 6.7 g fibre, 19.2 g protein, 0.5 g salt

Weekday Meals

Super three-tomato sauce

The success of this richly flavoured tomato sauce relies on the quality of the raw ingredients as well as cooking it low and very slow – the longer you cook the sauce, the richer and more intensely flavoured it becomes. I like to make this sauce in bulk and freeze it in portions. It's excellent served just as it is, slightly chunky, or strained and smooth. Serve it with pasta or, alternatively, use as a base sauce for meat, poultry, seafood or vegetables.

4 tablespoons olive oil
2 onions, finely chopped
3 large garlic cloves, finely chopped
700 g/1 lb. 9 oz. vine-ripened tomatoes, cut into thin wedges, retaining the vines
2 x 400 g/14 oz. cans plum tomatoes
60 g/2¼ oz. sun-dried tomatoes in oil, drained and roughly chopped
15 g/½ oz. basil sprigs
sea salt and cracked black pepper

Low 9–10 hours

Makes about 1–1.5 litres/5–5½ cups

Heat the oil in a saucepan, add the onions and cook over a medium-low heat for 10 minutes until softened. Add the garlic and fresh tomatoes and cook for a minute or so, gently crushing the tomatoes with the back of a spatula.

Transfer the onion mixture to the slow cooker pot with the canned plum tomatoes, sun-dried tomatoes, basil and the reserved vines from the fresh tomatoes, if you have them. Cover and cook on low for 9–10 hours. Season with salt and pepper.

For a chunky sauce, remove the vines and roughly mash the sauce in the slow cooker using a potato masher. For a smooth sauce, pass it through a sieve/strainer into a bowl; it's easier to do this a couple of ladlefuls at a time. Take your time pressing the tomatoes through the sieve/strainer to extract all the goodness and occasionally discard any skin and seeds that build up in the sieve/strainer. The sauce is ready to use as you wish or it can be left to cool and chilled for up to 3 days or frozen.

NUTRITIONAL INFORMATION
108 kcals, 7.1 g fat (1g saturates), 7.9 g carbohydrate (7.1 g sugars), 2.5 g fibre, 1.8 g protein, 0.2 g salt (based on 100 ml/⅓ cup serving)

Weekday tagine

Packed with good-for-you vegetables and pulses, this hearty Moroccan tagine is both sustaining and filling and is just the thing for a warming midweek meal. The cauliflower is lightly cooked, so it retains its texture and valuable nutrients, including vitamin C, folate and phytonutrients. I've used canned chickpeas/garbanzo beans to avoid having to soak and pre-boil them first but if you prefer dried, a can is the equivalent of around 200 g/1 cup dried.

2 tablespoons olive oil
1 large onion, finely chopped
4 carrots, diced
3 garlic cloves, chopped
400 g/14 oz. can chickpeas/garbanzo beans, drained
55 g/¼ cup dried Puy lentils, rinsed
1 tablespoon ras-el-hanout
1 teaspoon turmeric powder
1 teaspoon ground ginger
½ teaspoon dried chilli/red pepper flakes
4 dried dates, roughly chopped
2 tablespoons tomato purée/paste
375 ml/1½ cups hot vegetable stock
1 unwaxed lemon, cut in half
2 handfuls chopped parsley
½ small cauliflower, grated or blitzed in a food processor
sea salt and cracked black pepper
pomegranate and wholewheat couscous, to serve

Low 7–8 hours
High 4–5 hours

Serves 4

Put all the ingredients up to and including the hot vegetable stock into the slow cooker pot. Stir well until combined and add the lemon halves, pressing them into the pot.

Cover and cook on low for 7–8 hours, or high for 4–5 hours. Remove the lemon halves, stir in half the parsley and the cauliflower, season with salt and pepper, and add more hot stock or water, if needed, to make a sauce-like consistency. Cover and cook for another 15 minutes – the cauliflower just needs to soften in the residual heat.

Scatter the remaining parsley and the pomegranate over the tagine and serve with couscous.

NUTRITIONAL INFORMATION
301 kcals, 9.2 g fat (1.3 g saturates), 35.1 g carbohydrate (20.3 g sugars), 11.8 g fibre, 11.8 g protein, 0.8 g salt

Black lentil dhal with beetroot/beet raita

Perfect comfort food, this hearty dhal is similar to the classic Punjabi *dal makhani*, but uses green lentils instead of the more usual red kidney beans. The benefits of using dried green lentils alongside the urad dhal (black lentils) is that neither need pre-soaking or cooking, so you can assemble the ingredients and turn on the slow cooker first thing and you'll be welcomed home with the wonderful aroma of dhal. The vibrant pink beetroot/beet raita adds a vibrant colour contrast to the black lentils as well as useful amounts of iron and folate.

1 tablespoon ghee or coconut oil
1 large onion, finely chopped
3 garlic cloves, finely chopped
4-cm/1½-in. piece root ginger, grated
2 teaspoons cumin seeds
1 medium-sized green chilli/chile, deseeded and finely chopped
3 cardamom pods, split
1 small cinnamon stick
1 teaspoon turmeric
200 g/1 cup whole black lentils (urad dahl), rinsed
55 g/¼ cup dried green lentils, rinsed
2 teaspoons vegetable bouillon powder
good squeeze of lemon juice
1 handful coriander/cilantro, to serve
wholewheat chapattis, to serve

BEETROOT/BEET RAITA

1 raw beetroot/beet, grated
100 g/3½ oz. white cabbage, shredded
1 carrot, grated
1 small eating apple, cored and grated
juice of 1 small lemon
½ small red onion, diced
100 ml/½ cup live plain yogurt
sea salt and cracked black pepper

Low 7–8 hours
High 5–6 hours

Serves 4

Put all the ingredients up to and including the green lentils in the slow cooker pot. Pour in 700 ml/3 cups hot water and stir until combined and the ghee or coconut oil melts.

Cover and cook on low for 7–8 hours, or high for 5–6 hours, until the lentils are tender.

To make the beetroot/beet raita, mix together all the ingredients in a bowl and season.

Just before serving the dhal, stir the bouillon powder into the dhal and add a good squeeze of lemon juice. Add a splash more hot water if it's too dry – you want it to have a thick, soupy consistency – or if too wet, take off the lid and cook on high for 15 minutes. Taste and add extra salt and pepper, if needed.

Serve the dhal in shallow bowls, topped with a spoonful of the beetroot/beet raita and a sprinkling of coriander/cilantro, with warm chapattis by the side.

NUTRITIONAL INFORMATION
275 kcals, 4.6 g fat (3g saturates),
33.8 g carbohydrate (4.7 g sugars), 12.4 g fibre,
18.5 g protein, 1.4 g salt

Mediterranean vegetables with preserved lemons

The Mediterranean diet has long been reputed to be life enhancing. New research confirms that not only is it a way of eating that's good for the heart, it may also reduce the risk of type-2 diabetes and other chronic long-term diseases. This light, summery stew is packed with good-for-you ingredients. The dried kombu seaweed is optional; it helps to soften the beans during cooking as well as adding a wealth of minerals – iodine, iron, calcium, magnesium – to the dish.

200 g/1 cup dried haricot beans/navy beans, soaked overnight
1 tablespoon olive oil
1 large onion, thinly sliced
2 garlic cloves, finely chopped
1 large red (bell) pepper, deseeded and thinly sliced
1 large fennel bulb, sliced
5 sun-dried tomatoes in oil, chopped, plus 1 tablespoon oil from the jar
1 medium-sized red chilli/chile, deseeded and diced
1½ teaspoons dried thyme
3 long basil sprigs
1 teaspoon turmeric

1 piece of kombu, soaked in hot water for 20 minutes (optional)
1 teaspoon bouillon powder
3 courgettes/zucchini, cut into half-moons
1 small preserved lemon, flesh discarded, skin finely chopped
sea salt and cracked black pepper
wholewheat couscous, chopped parsley and Lemon Tahini Sauce (see page 59) (optional), to serve

Low 7–8 hours
High 4–5 hours

Serves 4

Drain and rinse the soaked beans and tip them into a large saucepan. Cover with plenty of cold water and bring to the boil. Let the beans boil rapidly for 10 minutes, then turn the heat down and simmer for another 10 minutes. Drain the beans, discarding the cooking water, and tip them into the slow cooker pot.

Add the oil, onion, garlic, red (bell) pepper, fennel, sun-dried tomatoes and their oil, chilli/chile, herbs, turmeric, kombu and 500 ml/2 cups hot water to the pot. Cover and cook on low for 7–8 hours, or high for 4–5 hours, until the beans are tender.

An hour before serving, stir in the bouillon powder, courgettes/zucchini and preserved lemon, stir briefly until combined and cover with the lid to continue cooking. Season with salt and pepper and serve with couscous, sprinkled with parsley, and the Lemon Tahini Sauce, if liked.

NUTRITIONAL INFORMATION
280 kcals, 8.1 g fat (1.3 g saturates), 34.6 g carbohydrate (11.3 g sugars), 7.1 g fibre, 15 g protein, 1.7 g salt

Restorative chicken miso broth

Good for the soul, heart and digestion, this Japanese-style broth is flavoured with ginger, garlic and miso. The miso is best added towards the end of the cooking time since its nutrients, beneficial bacteria and enzymes are sensitive to heat.

1 large onion, cut into thin wedges
1 celery stick, sliced
2 carrots, sliced
1.3 kg/3 lb. free-range chicken
1 unwaxed lemon, cut in half
3 star anise
3 large garlic cloves, peeled and left whole
7-cm/2¾-in. piece root ginger, sliced
10 peppercorns
4 tablespoons brown rice miso
2 teaspoons tamari or reduced-salt soy sauce
4 spring onions/scallions, thinly sliced diagonally
125 g/4½ oz. asparagus tips, trimmed
200 g/7 oz. wholemeal noodles
4 handfuls watercress
1 tablespoon toasted sesame seeds
sea salt

Low 7 hours, plus 20 minutes on high
High 4½ hours

Serves 4

Put the onion, celery and carrots in the slow cooker pot. Insert the lemon halves inside the chicken carcass and place it on top of the vegetables, then pour in 700 ml/3 cups hot water. Scatter the star anise, garlic, ginger and peppercorns around the chicken, making sure they are immersed in the water. Cover and cook on low for 7 hours, or high for 4 hours, until the chicken is cooked through and the juices run clear when the thickest part of the thigh is pierced with a skewer. Remove the chicken, place on a warmed plate and cover with foil.

Using a slotted spoon, lift out the flavourings into a sieve/strainer set over a bowl. Stir the miso and tamari or soy sauce into the flavoured stock, then add the white parts of the spring onions/scallions and the asparagus. Turn to high if on low. Cover and cook for another 20 minutes or until the asparagus is tender.

Meanwhile, pick out and discard the ginger, peppercorns and star anise from the sieve/strainer and press the vegetables through the sieve/strainer with the back of a spoon into the bowl. Quickly stir the vegetable purée into the stock and replace the lid.

Cook the noodles in a separate saucepan following the packet instructions. Carve the chicken, discarding the skin, then shred the meat into long strips. You should have some chicken left over – leave it to cool and store in the fridge for up to 3 days. To serve, divide the chicken and noodles between four bowls. Ladle the vegetables and stock over. Top with the watercress, the green parts of the spring onions/scallions and sesame seeds.

NUTRITIONAL INFORMATION
477 kcals, 8.1 g fat (2.3 g saturates), 53 g carbohydrate (11.3 g sugars), 9.3 g fibre, 45 g protein, 2.9 g salt

Salmon parcels
with quick cucumber pickle

Slow cookers are perfect for cooking fish, especially slightly firmer fillets, cooking them gently and slowly. I'd usually recommend using salmon steaks here, as they seem to hold their form better but since the fish are contained within a parcel, fillets are just fine – lightly smoked salmon works well, too. Nutritionally, salmon is an excellent source of good-quality protein, vitamins B12, B6 and D and the mineral, selenium, but as part of the oily fish family its omega-3 content is the focus of most attention for its contribution to a healthy brain, heart and joints.

4 wild salmon fillets, skin on
1 large lemon, cut into 8 slices
sea salt and cracked black pepper
rye bread, or gluten-free alternative, and a mixed leaf salad with radish sprouts, to serve

QUICK CUCUMBER PICKLE
2 tablespoons apple cider vinegar
1 teaspoon raw honey
½ teaspoon sea salt
10-cm/4-in. piece cucumber, sliced into thin rounds
1 teaspoon nori flakes, for sprinkling

Low 2–2³⁄₄ hours
High 45 minutes–
   1¼ hours

Serves 4

Pat dry the salmon fillets with paper towels and place each one on a sheet of foil large enough to make a parcel. Season with salt and pepper and place 2 lemon slices on top of each one. Fold up the sides of the foil to make a parcel, place in the slow cooker pot and repeat to make four parcels in total.

Cover and cook on low for 2–2¾ hours, or high for 45 minutes–1¼ hours, until the fish is opaque and flaky.

While the fish is cooking, make the quick cucumber pickle. Mix together the vinegar, honey and salt in a bowl until the salt dissolves. Stir in the cucumber then massage it with your fingers until it starts to soften. Leave for 15 minutes to let the cucumber take on the flavours of the pickle, then spoon into a serving bowl and sprinkle over the nori flakes.

Open the parcels and place the salmon on serving plates, pour over any juices left in the foil. Serve the fish with the pickle, rye bread and a mixed leaf and radish sprout salad.

NUTRITIONAL INFORMATION
270 kcals, 14.4 g fat (3 g saturates), 2.9 g carbohydrate
(2.9 g sugars), 0.6 g fibre 31.6 g protein, 0.9 g salt

Jamaican black bean pot

If the beans are pre-soaked and part-cooked, this vibrant stew with its mix of black beans, red and yellow (bell) peppers and orange squash, can be put on first thing and will be perfect by dinner time. Don't add salt or the bouillon powder until the end of the cooking time since they will toughen the beans. Chilli/Chile Cornbread (see page 31), brown rice or quinoa are all perfect sides.

200 g/²/₃ cup dried black beans, soaked overnight
1 tablespoon ghee or coconut oil
1 large onion, finely chopped
350 g/12 oz. peeled, deseeded butternut squash, cut into small pieces
1 red and 1 yellow (bell) pepper, deseeded and cut into small pieces
4 garlic cloves, chopped
2 teaspoons English mustard powder
2 teaspoons blackstrap molasses
1 teaspoon raw honey
2 teaspoons dried thyme
½–1 teaspoon dried chilli/red pepper flakes, to taste
1 heaped teaspoon bouillon powder
juice of 1 lime
sea salt and cracked black pepper
rocket/arugula leaves, avocado and lime wedges, to serve

Low 7–8 hours
High 5–6 hours

Serves 4

Drain and rinse the soaked beans. Put them in a saucepan, cover with plenty of cold water and bring to the boil. Let the beans boil rapidly for 10 minutes then turn the heat down and simmer for another 10 minutes, drain and discard the cooking water.

While the beans are cooking, heat the ghee or coconut oil in a large frying pan/skillet, add the onion and fry for 8 minutes until softened, then stir in the squash, (bell) peppers and garlic and cook for another couple of minutes.

Tip the onion mixture into the slow cooker pot and stir in the mustard, molasses, honey, thyme, chilli/red pepper flakes, part-cooked black beans and 500 ml/2 cups hot water. Cover and cook on low for 7–8 hours, or high for 5–6 hours, until the beans and squash are tender. Just before serving, stir in the bouillon powder and the lime juice and season with salt and pepper.

Spoon the black beans into four serving bowls and top with a handful of rocket/arugula leaves and sliced avocado and serve with wedges of lime for squeezing over.

NUTRITIONAL INFORMATION
301 kcals, 4.9 g fat (3.1 g saturates), 46 g carbohydrate (15.7 g sugars), 8.9 g fibre, 15.3 g protein, 1.4 g salt

Sea bass in chilli/chile tomato sauce

The premise behind the recipes in this chapter is simplicity and convenience so, for many of us, that means a slow-cooked dish that can be put on in the morning and be ready by dinner. This cooking method works with some ingredients better than others, seafood and delicate vegetables being two that are more tricky to get right since timing can be more of an issue. This recipe fits the brief perfectly – the sauce is cooked slowly throughout the day, while the sea bass is added to the slow cooker closer to serving so the fish remains moist and flaky. Serve this with plenty of steamed green vegetables.

400 g/14 oz. can chopped tomatoes
1 small red onion, finely diced
2 garlic cloves, thinly sliced
2 anchovies in oil, drained and finely chopped
2 teaspoons capers, rinsed, patted dry and chopped
125 g/4½ oz. roasted red (bell) peppers from a jar, sliced
1 medium-sized red chilli/chile, deseeded and finely chopped
700 g/1 lb. 9 oz. new potatoes, scrubbed and quartered

1 tablespoon tomato purée/paste
few sprigs lemon thyme or 1 teaspoon dried thyme
4 large sea bass fillets
4 lemon slices, plus an extra squeeze
2 bay leaves
chopped parsley, to serve (optional)
sea salt and cracked black pepper

Low 7–8 hours
High 4–5 hours

Serves 4

Put the chopped tomatoes, onion, garlic, anchovies, capers, red (bell) peppers, chilli/chile, new potatoes, tomato purée/paste, 5 tablespoons water and lemon thyme in the slow cooker pot. Cover and cook on low for 7 hours, or high for 4 hours, until the potatoes are tender when pierced with a fork.

Place two slices of lemon and a bay leaf on one of the sea bass fillets, season with salt and pepper and place a second fillet on top to form a sea bass 'sandwich', with the skin facing outwards. Repeat with the two remaining fillets. Place the fish on top of the tomato sauce, cover and cook for 40 minutes–1 hour until the fish is opaque and flaky.

To serve, carefully remove the fish from the pot. Add a squeeze of lemon juice to the sauce, season with salt and pepper, and spoon it into serving bowls. Top with a sea bass fillet and scatter over some chopped parsley, if you like, before serving.

NUTRITIONAL INFORMATION
297 kcals, 3.2 g fat (0.8 g saturates), 34.9 g carbohydrate (10.9 g sugars), 5.3 g fibre, 29 g protein, 0.7 g salt

Mackerel with mango salsa

I've found that wrapping the mackerel in individual foil parcels is the easiest way to cook the fish in a slow cooker. Additionally, the parcels keep the fish moist and have the added bonus of reducing any fishy aromas. Mackerel is economical to buy and is packed with beneficial omega-3 fatty acids, which have been linked to improved heart health and reduced inflammation in the body. The vitamin C-rich salsa adds a fresh, zingy note.

4 whole mackerel, gutted, cleaned, heads removed
1 lime, thinly sliced
2 lemongrass stalks, outer leaves removed, cut in half and flattened with the side of a knife
sea salt and cracked black pepper
salad leaves and crusty bread, to serve

HOT MANGO SALSA
1 mango, skin and stone/pit removed, flesh diced
½ red onion, diced
2 handfuls chopped coriander/cilantro
juice of 1 lime
½ medium-sized red chilli/chile, deseeded and diced
1 tablespoon extra virgin olive oil, plus extra for drizzling

Low 1½–2 hours, depending on the size of the fish

Serves 4

Rinse and pat dry the mackerel. Place each fish on a sheet of foil large enough to make a parcel. Stuff each fish with a couple of slices of lime and a crushed lemongrass stick. Drizzle over a little olive oil and season with salt and pepper. Gather up and fold the sides of the foil to make four sealed parcels.

Put the foil-wrapped fish in the slow cooker pot, arranging them on top of one another, if necessary. I'd also recommend any larger fish be placed on the bottom layer. Cover and cook on low for 1½–2 hours, depending on how large the fish are. To check the fish are cooked without losing too much heat in the slow cooker, remove a parcel, replacing the lid, unwrap slightly and check the thickest part of the fish to see if the flesh is opaque and flaky. If the fish isn't quite ready, return it to the slow cooker, taking care not to leave the lid off for too long.

While the fish is cooking, mix together all the ingredients for the hot mango salsa, reserving half of the coriander/cilantro for sprinkling over at the end. Season and set aside. Open up the foil parcels, place the fish on serving plates and remove the stuffing ingredients. Serve the mackerel with the salsa, salad leaves and bread by the side. Sprinkle over the reserved coriander/cilantro just before serving.

NUTRITIONAL INFORMATION
522 kcals, 38.6 g fat (8.5 g saturates), 9.9 g carbohydrate (9 g sugars), 2.3 g fibre, 32.7 g protein, 0.8 g salt

Korean shiitake and noodle bowl with crispy tofu

South Korean cooking is big on immune-supporting and digestion-enhancing fermented foods. Kombu seaweed is rich in minerals such as calcium, iron, magnesium, potassium and iodine.

15 g/½ oz. dried shiitake mushrooms

5-cm/2-in. piece root ginger, thinly sliced

10-cm/4-in. piece dried kombu, rinsed

2 large garlic cloves, thinly sliced

½ teaspoon gochujang or hot chilli/chile sauce

125 g/1 cup shelled edamame beans, defrosted if frozen

200 g/7 oz. long-stem broccoli

240 g/8½ oz. wholewheat noodles

6 spring onions/ scallions, thinly sliced diagonally

1 teaspoon toasted sesame seeds

kimchi, to serve (optional)

CRISPY TOFU

300 g/10½ oz. firm tofu, drained well

4 tablespoons white miso

1 teaspoon sesame oil

1 tablespoon reduced-salt soy sauce, plus extra to serve

2 tablespoons cold-pressed rapeseed oil

Low 3 hours, plus 20 minutes on high

High 2½ hours

Serves 4

For the crispy tofu, drain the tofu on paper towels then cut it into 1 cm/½ in. thick slices. Mix together the miso, sesame oil and soy sauce in a shallow dish. Add the tofu, turn to coat and leave to marinate in the fridge.

Soak the dried shiitake for 15 minutes in 100 ml/ ⅓ cup just-boiled water until softened. Put the shiitake and the soaking liquid into the slow cooker pot with the ginger and kombu and 700 ml/3 cups hot water. Cover and cook on low for 3 hours, or high for 2 hours. Remove and discard the ginger and kombu.

Meanwhile, continue with the tofu. Heat the oil in a large frying pan/skillet over a medium-high heat, remove the tofu from the marinade and fry it for 10–12 minutes, turning once, until crisp and golden. Drain the tofu on paper towels.

Stir any marinade left in the bowl into the slow cooker pot with the garlic, gochujang or chilli/chile sauce, edamame and broccoli. Cover, turn the temperature to high, and cook for 15–20 minutes until the broccoli is just tender. Cook the noodles according to the packet instructions. Drain and divide them between four bowls and scatter over the spring onions/ scallions. Ladle the vegetable broth over the noodles and finish with a topping of tofu and sesame seeds if using.

NUTRITIONAL INFORMATION
501 kcals, 17.5 g fat (2.1 g saturates), 58 g carbohydrate (5.4 g sugars), 10.4 g fibre, 27.2 g protein, 3.3 g salt

Lemon chicken pilaf

Fragrant and lemony, this one-pot meal is easily adaptable – so do use your favourite spices and additions so long as the rice remains at the heart of the dish. If you can't find boneless chicken thighs, buy them bone-on then slice off the meat and retain the larger bones to add to the pilaf at the start of the cooking time for extra flavour and goodness – do make sure you remove them before serving. Opt for easy-cook/quick cooking brown rice since it retains its texture, separate grains and slight bite when cooked in the slow cooker.

1 tablespoon olive oil
1 large onion, finely chopped
2 teaspoons cumin seeds
2 teaspoons coriander seeds
3 garlic cloves, finely chopped
6 skinless, boneless large chicken thighs, cut into bite-sized pieces
250 g/1¼ cups easy-cook/quick cooking brown rice
600 ml/2½ cups hot chicken stock
1 heaped teaspoon turmeric powder
1 small cinnamon stick
4 cardamom pods, split
70 g/⅓ cup unsulphured chopped dried apricots
1 unwaxed lemon, cut in half
3 good handfuls spinach, leaves shredded
sea salt and cracked black pepper
hummus or live plain yogurt, and toasted pumpkin seeds, to serve

Low 3–4 hours
High 2–2½ hours

Serves 4

Heat the oil in a large frying pan/skillet, add the onion and fry for 10 minutes until softened. Using a pestle and mortar, grind the cumin and coriander seeds and add them to the pan with the garlic and cook for another minute. Stir the chicken and rice into the pan and stir until everything is combined.

Transfer the rice mixture to the slow cooker pot, pour in the stock and stir in the turmeric, cinnamon, cardamom and apricots. Add lemon halves, pressing them into the rice mixture. Cover and cook on low for 3–4 hours, or high for 2–2½ hours, until the rice has absorbed the stock and is tender but still retains a little bite.

Turn the slow cooker off, stir in the spinach and let it soften in the residual heat for 5–10 minutes until wilted but it still retains its colour. Season with salt and pepper.

Serve the rice in bowls, removing the cinnamon stick and cardamom pods. Top with a good spoonful of hummus or yogurt and a sprinkling of pumpkin seeds.

NUTRITIONAL INFORMATION
554 kcals, 15.8 g fat (3.9 g saturates), 60 g carbohydrate (15 g sugars), 9.8 g fibre, 37.2 g protein, 5 g salt

Jerk chicken tacos

Chicken is a great source of good-quality, low-fat protein. The marinade helps to keep the meat moist as it cooks.

2 red onions

1 medium-sized red chilli/ chile, deseeded and roughly chopped

2.5-cm/1-in. piece root ginger

1 large garlic clove, chopped

1 tablespoon balsamic vinegar

juice of 2 limes

1 tablespoon allspice

1 teaspoon cayenne pepper

2 teaspoons dried thyme

8 chicken thighs on the bone, skin removed

1 tablespoon olive oil

sea salt and cracked black pepper

TO SERVE

1 large avocado, cut in half, stone/pit removed, peeled and diced

1 handful chopped coriander/cilantro leaves

3 vine-ripened tomatoes, deseeded and diced

1 tablespoon extra virgin olive oil

4 corn tortillas, warmed

4 handfuls rocket/arugula leaves

Low 7–8 hours
High 3–5 hours

Serves 4

Chop a quarter of the onions and place it in a mini food processor or blender with the chilli/chile, ginger, garlic, balsamic vinegar and juice of 1 lime and then blitz to a coarse paste. Stir in the allspice, cayenne pepper and thyme, and season with salt and pepper. Spread the paste all over the chicken thighs. Place on a plate, cover with clingfilm/plastic wrap, and leave to marinate in the fridge for a few hours, or overnight if time.

Cut the remaining whole onion into horizontal slices and place in the base of the slow cooker pot, then arrange the marinated chicken thighs on top, spooning over any residual marinade left on the plate. Cover and cook on low for 7–8 hours, or high for 3–5 hours, until cooked through.

Remove the chicken, then pull the meat away from the bones. Cover with foil to keep it warm. Discard the bones.

Scoop off any fat on the surface of the gravy and turn the slow cooker to high if on low. Using a slotted spoon or skimmer, remove the onion to a sieve/strainer set over a bowl. Press the onion through the sieve/strainer into the bowl with the back of a spoon. Stir the onion paste into the gravy in the pot and cook, uncovered, for 10 minutes or so until reduced.

While the gravy is cooking, finely chop the remaining onion and place in a bowl with the avocado, coriander/cilantro, tomatoes and the remaining lime juice. Season and stir gently until combined.

Arrange the chicken on the warmed tortillas, pour over a little of the reduced gravy, just enough to moisten the chicken, and top with a handful of rocket/arugula leaves and the avocado mixture.

NUTRITIONAL INFORMATION
613 kcals, 29.9 g fat (7.7 g saturates), 39.8 g carbohydrate (9.1 g sugars), 6.1 g fibre, 43 g protein, 1.5 g salt

Red cooked chicken

This Chinese-style dish requires very little in the way of pre-preparation – just chuck everything in the slow cooker and you're good to go. If you haven't come across kuzu before, it's a gluten-free thickener made from plant roots and can be used in exactly the same way as cornflour/cornstarch. In addition to its excellent thickening properties, kuzu is said to be good for calming the digestive system as well as treating headaches and the common cold.

2.5-cm/1-in. piece root ginger, grated

3 tablespoons reduced-salt soy sauce

1 tablespoon raw honey

3 garlic cloves, finely chopped

1 teaspoon sesame oil

1 tablespoon rice vinegar or apple cider vinegar

1 teaspoon Chinese five spice

1½ teaspoons chilli/chile sauce

700 g/1 lb. 9 oz. boneless, skinless chicken thighs, cut into large bite-sized chunks

6 spring onions/scallions, sliced diagonally

1½ tablespoons kuzu or cornflour/cornstarch

200 g/7 oz. long-stem broccoli

cracked black pepper

2 teaspoons toasted sesame seeds, chopped coriander/cilantro, lime wedges and brown rice, to serve

Low 6 hours, plus 1 hour on high
High 4½ hours

Serves 4

Mix together the ginger, soy sauce, honey, garlic, sesame oil, rice vinegar or cider vinegar, Chinese five spice and chilli/chile sauce in the slow cooker pot. Stir in the chicken until evenly coated in the mixture.

Cover and cook on low for 6 hours, or high for 3 hours. Scoop out the chicken with a slotted spoon onto a plate and cover with foil to keep it warm while you thicken the sauce. Stir the kuzu or cornflour/cornstarch into a little water and add to the pot. Turn the slow cooker to high if cooking on low, and cook for 15 minutes, stirring until the sauce has thickened.

Return the chicken to the pot with the white part of the spring onions/scallions, stir until coated in the sauce. Cover and cook on high for another 1 hour, until the chicken is tender and the sauce is rich and sticky.

Just before the chicken is ready, steam the broccoli and divide it between serving plates then top with the chicken. Spoon the sauce over and sprinkle with sesame seeds, the green parts of the spring onions/scallions and the coriander/cilantro. Serve with lime wedges and rice by the side.

NUTRITIONAL INFORMATION
350 kcals, 14 g fat (3.9 g saturates), 16.2 g carbohydrate (10.8 g sugars), 2.7 g fibre, 37.2 g protein, 1.7 g salt

Brazilian chicken and sweet potato curry

I love the simplicity of the spicing in this curry, yet it's still packed with flavour. Turmeric, fresh root or in powdered form, is the superfood of the moment with a long list of impressive attributes. Its active ingredient curcumin is a powerful antioxidant and anti-inflammatory and is reputed to help fight many chronic diseases, from heart disease to cancer.

2 onions, coarsely grated

4 garlic cloves, coarsely grated

5-cm/2-in. piece root ginger, finely chopped

1½ teaspoons hot cayenne pepper

900 g/2 lb. skinless chicken thighs on the bone

1 tablespoon coconut oil or ghee

1 large red (bell) pepper, deseeded and chopped

1 medium-sized red chilli/chile, deseeded and finely chopped

450 g/1 lb. sweet potatoes, peeled and cut into chunks

2 tablespoons tomato purée/paste

1 teaspoon turmeric

400 g/14 oz. can coconut milk

2 tomatoes, deseeded and diced

85 g/3 oz. curly kale, leaves finely chopped

sea salt and cracked black pepper

chopped coriander/ cilantro, black rice and lime wedges, to serve

Low 5–6 hours
High 4–5 hours

Serves 4

Mix together half the onion, garlic and ginger and all of the cayenne pepper in a large bowl, season with salt and pepper and stir in the chicken thighs. Cover and leave the chicken to marinate in the fridge for 2 hours or overnight.

Heat the coconut oil or ghee in a large frying pan/skillet, add the remaining onion, garlic and ginger and fry for 5 minutes, until softened. Tip the onion mixture into the slow cooker pot and add the red (bell) pepper, chilli/chile, sweet potatoes, tomato purée/paste, turmeric, coconut milk and tomatoes. Stir well until combined, then press the chicken into the sauce. Cover and cook on low for 5–6 hours, or high for 4–5 hours, until the chicken is cooked.

Twenty minutes before serving, turn the heat to high if it's on low and stir in the kale. Remove the chicken thighs from the sauce, pull the meat off the bones in pieces and return it to the sauce, discarding the bones. Season with salt and pepper, and serve with coriander/cilantro leaves, black rice and wedges of lime for squeezing over.

NUTRITIONAL INFORMATION
547 kcals, 30.1 g fat (20.9 g saturates), 36.1 g carbohydrate (18 g sugars), 7.9 g fibre, 27.6 g protein, 0.6 g salt

Beef and aubergine/eggplant stifado

If you've travelled to Greece, you may be familiar with stifado, a richly flavoured stew that's a regular on taverna menus. This version uses a smaller amount of beef than usual, supplementing it with a nutritious combination of aubergine/eggplant, green lentils and butter/lima beans. If I'm serving this for a weekday meal, I prepare the stifado the night before and simply turn the slow cooker on before work in the morning.

400 g/14 oz. braising/chuck steak, trimmed of fat, cut into bite-sized chunks

3 tablespoons olive oil

1 aubergine/eggplant, diced

1 large onion, finely chopped

175 ml/³⁄4 cup red wine (optional)

4 garlic cloves, finely chopped

700 ml/3³⁄4 cups passata/tomato sauce

1 tablespoon tomato purée/paste

2 tablespoons apple cider vinegar

2 teaspoons dried oregano

1 small cinnamon stick

3 cloves, tied in a muslin/cheesecloth bag

70 g/¹⁄2 cup pitted black olives

400 g/14 oz. can butter/lima beans, drained

400 g/14 oz. can green lentils, drained

sea salt and cracked black pepper

Courgette/Zucchini Tzatziki (see page 56), to serve

Low 7–8 hours
High 5–6 hours

Serves 4

Season the beef with salt and pepper. Heat 1 tablespoon of the oil in a sauté pan/skillet, add the beef and cook until browned all over. Remove with a slotted spoon, then heat the remaining oil in the pan. Add the aubergine/eggplant and onion and fry for 10 minutes until softened and golden.

Return the beef to the pan and pour in the red wine, if using. Let the wine bubble away until completely evaporated and there is no smell of alcohol – this is important as the wine will not cook down in the slow cooker and you'll be left with a strong flavour of alcohol.

Tip the beef mixture into the slow cooker pot and stir in the garlic, passata/tomato sauce, tomato purée/paste, apple cider vinegar, oregano, cinnamon, cloves, olives and butter/lima beans. Cover and cook on low for 7–8 hours, or high for 5–6 hours, adding the lentils 1 hour before the end of the cooking time. Remove the cinnamon and clove bag and season with salt and pepper. Serve topped with a spoonful of courgette/zucchini tzatziki.

NUTRITIONAL INFORMATION
503 kcals, 18.5 g fat (4.2 g saturates), 34.5 g carbohydrate (16.6 g sugars), 10.9 g fibre, 36 g protein, 1 g salt

Oriental beef, orange and star anise pot

Red meat, although not an essential part of a healthy diet, does provide beneficial amounts of iron, vitamin B12 and zinc, nutrients that can be lacking in an unbalanced vegetarian diet. Brisket and braising steak are relatively cheap cuts, but buy the best quality you can afford from grass-fed, organic cows. The quantity of beef is kept low and is supplemented by a healthy amount of vegetables. Cooked slowly in a Chinese-inspired sauce flavoured with orange juice, Chinese five spice and star anise, the stew is rich and warming.

1 tablespoon spelt flour

2 tablespoons coconut oil or ghee

700 g/1 lb. 9 oz. beef brisket, fat trimmed, cut into bite-sized chunks

2 onions, thinly sliced

2 star anise

1 teaspoon Chinese five spice

5-cm/2-in. piece root ginger, thinly sliced

100 ml/⅓ cup fresh orange juice

3 tablespoons reduced-salt dark soy sauce or tamari

500 g/1 lb. 2 oz. butternut squash, peeled, deseeded and cut into bite-sized pieces

175 g/6 oz. long-stem broccoli

sea salt and cracked black pepper

brown basmati rice, to serve

Low 7–8 hours
High 5–6 hours

Serves 6

Season the flour with salt and pepper on a plate. Add the beef and turn to lightly coat it in the flour.

Heat half the coconut oil or ghee in a large frying pan/skillet. Add half the beef and cook until browned all over, about 10 minutes. Remove with a slotted spoon and set to one side, then brown the remaining beef, adding more oil or ghee, if needed. Return the beef to the pan, pour in 200 ml/¾ cup hot water and stir to remove any bits stuck to the bottom.

Transfer the beef and the liquid to the slow cooker pot and stir in the onions, star anise, five spice, ginger, orange juice, soy sauce and squash.

Cover and cook on low for 7–8 hours, or high for 5–6 hours, until the squash and beef are tender. 30 minutes before the end of the cooking time, add the broccoli, pushing it gently into the stew. Add a splash more hot water, if needed. Cover and cook until the broccoli is tender but still retains its colour. Season with salt and pepper and serve with steamed brown rice.

NUTRITIONAL INFORMATION
547 kcals, 30.1 g fat (20.9 g saturates), 36.1 g carbohydrate (18 g sugars), 7.9 g fibre, 27.6 g protein, 0.6 g salt

Lamb, spelt and rosemary hotpot

Simply good, honest, homely food – the quantity of lamb in this hotpot is kept purposefully low, but there are lots of vegetables to boost its nutritional value and make sure you don't go hungry. Barley is just as good as spelt, here, but, whichever one you choose to use, make sure it's the pearled variety otherwise the grains can remain too firm and chewy.

2 tablespoons spelt flour

550 g/1 lb. 4 oz. lamb neck fillet, fat trimmed, cut into bite-sized chunks

2 tablespoons olive oil

850 ml/3½ cups hot beef stock

2 onions, finely chopped

2 carrots, diced

1 leek, sliced

1 celery stick, thinly sliced

200 g/7 oz. turnip, cut into small pieces

1 tablespoon finely chopped rosemary

2 teaspoons dried thyme

2 bay leaves

1 tablespoon English mustard

1 porcini stock cube, or 1 teaspoon vegetable bouillon powder

100 g/½ cup pearled spelt or barley, rinsed

2 handfuls cavolo nero, leaves finely chopped

sea salt and cracked black pepper

Low 7–8 hours
High 5–6 hours

Serves 4

Season the flour on a plate. Add the lamb and turn to coat it lightly in the seasoned flour. Heat the oil in a sauté pan/skillet, add the lamb and cook until browned all over, about 10 minutes.

Pour the beef stock into the pan and stir to remove any brown bits stuck on the bottom. Tip the lamb and stock into the slow cooker pot. Add the onions, carrots, leek, celery, turnip, herbs, mustard and porcini stock cube or vegetable bouillon. Stir in the spelt until combined. Cover and cook on low for 7–8 hours, or high for 5–6 hours, until the lamb and spelt are tender.

Twenty minutes before the end of the cooking time, stir in the cavolo nero (you can add an extra splash of hot water at this point if the hotpot looks dry). Cover and cook until the leaves are just tender.

NUTRITIONAL INFORMATION
594 kcals, 28.6 g fat (10.1 g saturates),
44 g carbohydrate (15.8 g sugars), 9.6 g fibre,
35.2 g protein, 2.7 g salt

Stuffed pork and chickpea/garbanzo bean tomatoes

Tomatoes are renowned for being the best source of lycopene, a powerful antioxidant that benefits the health of our bones and protects against DNA and cell damage. Here, tomatoes are filled with a nutritious mixture of lean mince/ground meat, chickpeas/garbanzo beans and wholewheat couscous.

4 medium-sized, vine-ripened beefsteak tomatoes

1 tablespoon olive oil, plus an extra splash

1 large onion, finely chopped

250 g/9 oz. lean pork or lamb mince/ground pork or lamb

3 garlic cloves, finely chopped

1 teaspoon ground allspice

2 teaspoons dried mint

100 g/½ cup (drained weight) canned chickpeas/garbanzo beans

2 tablespoons tomato purée/paste

50 g/⅓ cup wholewheat couscous

sea salt and cracked black pepper

Gremolata (see page 51) and mixed leaf salad, to serve

Low 2½–3 hours
High 1¾–2 hours

Serves 4

Slice the top 1 cm/½ in. off each tomato to make a lid. Using a teaspoon, scoop out the middle of the tomatoes, leaving a 1 cm/½ in. thick tomato 'basket'. Turn the tomatoes upside down on a plate to drain and reserve the tomato pulp and seeds.

Heat the oil in a large frying pan/skillet, add the onion and fry for 5 minutes until softened. Stir in the mince/ground pork or lamb, breaking it up with a spatula, and cook for another 10 minutes until it starts to brown. Stir in the garlic, allspice, mint, chickpeas/garbanzo beans, tomato purée/paste and couscous.

Strain the tomato juice and seeds through a sieve/strainer into a jug/pitcher, pressing the pulp with the back of a spoon to extract as much juice as possible; you need 100 ml/⅓ cup. Add the measured tomato juice to the meat mixture, stir until combined and season with salt and pepper.

Spoon the meat mixture into the hollowed-out tomatoes. Add a splash of oil to the slow cooker pot and arrange the tomatoes, ideally in a single layer, so they support each other securely. Top with the tomato 'lids'.

Cover and cook on low for 2½–3 hours, or high for 1¾–2 hours – the tomatoes should be tender but still hold their shape. Don't worry if they start to collapse a little as they still taste good. Serve the tomatoes topped with the gremolata with a mixed leaf salad by the side.

NUTRITIONAL INFORMATION
296 kcals, 10.6 g fat (2.7 g saturates), 28.1 g carbohydrate (14.4 g sugars), 6.6 g fibre, 18.2 g protein, 0.3 g salt

Slow Weekends

Slow-cooked onions with nut stuffing

Slow cooking does wonderful things to onions, turning them sweet, succulent and mellow. Onions have anti-inflammatory, immune-boosting and anti-carcinogenic properties – they are also easier to digest when cooked slowly if you have a sensitive gut. The onions are delicious served with the Super Three-Tomato Sauce (see page 70) or the Lemon Tahini Sauce (see page 59).

8 medium-sized onions, peeled
1 tablespoon olive oil
2 large garlic cloves, finely chopped
2 teaspoons dried thyme
2 tablespoons pumpkin seeds
2 tablespoons chopped walnuts
70 g/1⅓ cups day-old spelt breadcrumbs
70 g/2½ oz. sun-dried tomatoes in oil, finely chopped, plus 2 teaspoons oil for brushing
finely grated zest of 1 lemon
sea salt and cracked black pepper
chopped parsley, to serve

Low 5–6 hours
High 4–5 hours

Serves 6

Trim the root end of each onion to make a flat base. Using a small sharp knife, slice the top off each onion then cut out a deep hollow, leaving a 1.5 cm/¾ in. thick onion shell. Reserve half of the scooped-out onion (save the rest for another recipe) and finely chop.

Heat the olive oil in a large frying pan/skillet, add the chopped onion and fry for 8 minutes until softened. Add the garlic, thyme, pumpkin seeds and chopped walnuts and cook for another 2 minutes. Stir in the breadcrumbs, sun-dried tomatoes and lemon zest until combined. Season the stuffing mixture with salt and pepper.

Brush the outside of each onion with the oil from the sun-dried tomatoes. Generously fill each onion with the stuffing, pressing it down as you go and mounding the top.

Arrange the stuffed onions in the slow cooker pot – they should fit snugly. Cover and cook on low for 5–6 hours, or high for 4–5 hours. The onions should be beautifully tender but still keep their shape. Serve sprinkled with parsley.

NUTRITIONAL INFORMATION
250 kcals, 12.9 g fat (1.6 g saturates), 21.8 g carbohydrate (13.2 g sugars), 6.3 g fibre, 5.2 g protein, 0.4 g salt

Porcini and chestnut soup

Dried porcini may be a little pricey but you don't need a large quantity to add plenty of savoury, mushroomy flavour. High in fibre, chestnuts are a low glycaemic food, meaning they don't cause a spike in blood sugar levels. They also add to the rich flavour and texture of this thick, creamy soup. For a dairy-free soup add diced fresh pear and use hazelnut milk instead of crème fraiche.

25 g/1 oz. dried porcini
2 onions, finely chopped
1 celery stick, thinly sliced
2 large garlic cloves, finely chopped
2 bay leaves
1 porcini stock cube or 1 heaped teaspoon vegetable bouillon powder
300 g/10½ oz. potatoes, peeled and cut into small cubes
200 g/2 cups cooked whole chestnuts, chopped
2 teaspoons dried thyme
3 tablespoons crème fraiche
sea salt and cracked black pepper

TO SERVE
70 g/2½ oz. rindless goat's cheese, crumbled
2 tablespoons toasted pumpkin seeds
crusty spelt or rye bread, or gluten-free alternative

Low 5–6 hours
High 3–4 hours

Serves 4

Put two-thirds of the porcini in a bowl, cover with 100 ml/⅓ cup just-boiled water and leave to soak for 20 minutes until softened. Drain the porcini, reserving the soaking liquid, then finely chop the softened mushrooms.

Put the onions, celery, garlic, bay leaves, softened porcini and the reserved soaking liquid, potatoes, chestnuts and thyme in the slow cooker pot. Crumble the porcini stock cube (or stir the bouillon powder) into 850 ml/3½ cups hot water and add to the pot. Cover and cook on low for 5–6 hours, or high for 3–4 hours, until the potatoes and chestnuts are tender.

While the soup is cooking, put the remaining dried porcini in a grinder or use a pestle and mortar to grind to a powder. Leave to one side.

Remove the bay leaves and, using a stick blender, blend the soup until smooth. Stir in the crème fraiche and season with salt and pepper.

Ladle the soup into serving bowls then sprinkle over the goat's cheese, porcini powder and pumpkin seeds. Serve with slices of bread.

NUTRITIONAL INFORMATION
289 kcals, 11.1 g fat (6.5g saturates), 37.8 g carbohydrate (9.4 g sugars), 7.2 g fibre, 5.3 g protein, 0.9 g salt

Beetroot/beet, aduki bean and cacao chilli/chili

Packed with good-for-you ingredients, you get a triple dose of iron and a hefty helping of antioxidants from this chilli/chili, thanks to the addition of beetroot/beet, pulses and raw cacao. They also add to the slightly 'meaty' texture and colour of the chilli/chili, which is sure to win over any veggie sceptics. The raw cacao powder is stirred in towards the end of the cooking time to help retain its nutrient content.

150 g/¾ cup aduki beans, soaked overnight
50 g/¼ cup split red lentils, rinsed
1 tablespoon olive oil
1 large red onion, finely chopped
4 large garlic cloves, finely chopped
175 g/6 oz. raw beetroot/beets, peeled and diced
4-cm/1½-in. piece root ginger, grated
2 carrots
1 tablespoon chipotle chilli/chile paste or 1 tablespoon hot smoked paprika
½ teaspoon dried chilli/red pepper flakes

2 teaspoons cumin seeds
2 teaspoons dried oregano
400 g/14 oz. can chopped tomatoes
500 ml/2 cups hot vegetable stock
2 teaspoons raw cacao powder or cocoa powder
sea salt and cracked black pepper
baked sweet potatoes, soured cream, rocket/arugula and lemon wedges, to serve

Low 7–8 hours
High 5–6 hours

Serves 4

Put the soaked and drained aduki beans in a saucepan, cover with plenty of cold water and bring to the boil. Let the beans boil rapidly for 10 minutes then turn the heat down and simmer for another 10 minutes, drain and discard the cooking water.

Add the lentils, olive oil, onion, garlic, beetroot/beet, ginger, carrots, chipotle or smoked paprika, chilli/red pepper flakes, cumin, oregano, chopped tomatoes and stock to the pot with the beans, then stir until combined. Cover and cook on low for 7–8 hours, or high for 5–6 hours. Towards the end of the cooking time, stir in the cacao powder or cocoa and taste, adding more chilli/red pepper flakes, if you like your chilli/chili extra hot.

Season with salt and pepper and serve on a baked sweet potato with some soured cream, rocket/arugula leaves and lemon wedges by the side.

NUTRITIONAL INFORMATION
301 kcals, 5.9 g fat (1.6 g saturates), 43 g carbohydrate (15.3 g sugars), 11.1 g fibre, 15.4 g protein, 1.1 g salt

Whole sea bream with picada

A beautiful fish, sea bream has a slightly firm, flaky white flesh and is perfect for slow cooking. Here, the fish is served simply with the piquant Catalan-style sauce picada – a nutritious, lively blend of toasted nuts, herbs, garlic and lemon juice. Roasted new potatoes in their skins and steamed veg or salad make a wholesome meal with the bream.

4 medium-sized sea
   bream, gutted and
   cleaned, heads removed
1 lemon, thinly sliced into
   8 rounds
1 bunch flat-leaf parsley
15 g/⅛ stick unsalted
   butter, sliced into
   4 pieces
sea salt and cracked black
   pepper

PICADA
40 g/⅓ cup blanched
   almonds, toasted
1 small garlic clove, peeled
10 g/1 cup basil leaves
10 g/1 cup flat-leaf parsley
1 tablespoon capers,
   drained and patted dry
juice of 1 small lemon
6 tablespoons extra virgin
   olive oil

Low 1½–2 hours

Serves 4

Rinse and pat dry the sea bream. Place each one on a sheet of foil large enough to make a parcel. Stuff each fish with a couple of slices of lemon and a few sprigs of parsley. Top with a knob/pat of butter, season with salt and pepper, and gather up the sides of the foil to make four parcels.

Place the foil-wrapped fish in the slow cooker pot – they can be placed on top of one another, or overlapping, if needed. Cover and cook on low for 1½–2 hours, depending on the size of the fish. To check the fish are cooked, without losing too much heat in the slow cooker, remove one of the parcels, replacing the lid, open it up slightly and check the thickest part of the fish to see if the flesh is opaque and flaky. If the bream isn't quite ready, seal up the parcel and return it to the slow cooker, taking care not to leave the lid off for too long.

While the fish is cooking, make the picada. Put all the ingredients in a small blender (or use a tall beaker and a stick blender) and blend to a coarse paste – it should be similar in consistency to pesto. Season with salt and pepper and set aside.

When the fish is ready, open up the foil parcels and place on serving plates. Pour any buttery juices left in the foil over the fish and serve with the picada.

NUTRITIONAL INFORMATION
412 kcals, 31.9 g fat (5.1 g saturates), 2.4 g carbohydrate (1.9 g sugars), 2.3 g fibre, 27.5 g protein, 0.7 g salt

Spanish octopus with white beans and lemon

Baby octopus can be found ready-prepared and frozen in fishmongers or Asian supermarkets but if you have trouble finding them, squid is also excellent as are raw jumbo prawns/shrimp – they all take the same time to cook. (If using fresh rather than frozen seafood, you'll need about 225 g/8 oz.) This light, aromatic, nutritionally balanced stew is flavoured with smoked paprika, garlic, lemon and thyme. It couldn't be simpler to make – just place all the ingredients in the slow cooker pot and you're away. It's delicious served with farro, spelt or quinoa, or as part of a meze with crusty sourdough.

2 tablespoons olive oil, plus extra for drizzling

1 fennel bulb, thinly sliced crossways, fronds reserved

3 garlic cloves, finely chopped

280 g/10 oz. new potatoes, quartered

400 g/14 oz. can butter/lima beans, drained

175 g/6 oz. vine-ripened small tomatoes, deseeded and diced

2 tablespoons tomato purée/paste

1 tablespoon hot smoked paprika

2 teaspoons dried thyme

450 ml/1¾ cups hot fish stock

300 g/10½ oz. frozen prepared baby octopus or squid or prawns/shrimp, defrosted, drained well and patted dry

finely grated zest of ½ unwaxed lemon and juice of 1

sea salt and cracked black pepper

chopped parsley leaves, to serve

Low 6–7 hours, plus 30 minutes on high
High 4½–5½ hours

Serves 4

Put the olive oil, fennel, garlic, new potatoes, butter/lima beans, tomatoes, tomato purée/paste, smoked paprika and thyme in the slow cooker pot. Pour in the fish stock and stir gently until combined. Cover and cook on low for 6–7 hours, or high for 4–5 hours, until the potatoes are tender.

Turn the slow cooker to high if on low. Make sure the octopus is thoroughly drained and patted dry, otherwise it will make the sauce too watery, and add to the pot with the lemon zest and juice. Season with salt and pepper and turn briefly to coat the octopus in the sauce. Cover and cook for a further 25–30 minutes until the octopus is cooked and tender. Serve sprinkled with parsley and the reserved fennel fronds.

NUTRITIONAL INFORMATION
275 kcals, 8.8 g fat (1.4 g saturates),
23.6 g carbohydrate (6.6 g sugars), 6.9 g fibre,
22.1 g protein, 1 g salt

Pistachio-crusted salmon with tomatoes and artichokes

Slow-cooked until the vegetables almost start to break down, the sauce is delicious served on its own but tastes even better topped with the nut-crusted salmon fillets. The healthful combination of garlic, shallots, turmeric, squash, artichokes and tomatoes in the sauce provides a whole host of beneficial antioxidants, while the salmon is a well-known source of omega-3 fatty acids.

2 tablespoons olive oil
200 g/7 oz. shallots, thinly sliced
350 g/12 oz. butternut squash, peeled, deseeded and cut into small pieces
3 garlic cloves, finely chopped
1 teaspoon fennel seeds
150 g/5½ oz. chargrilled artichoke hearts in oil, halved if large
2 tablespoons tomato purée/paste
1 tablespoon capers, drained and chopped
1 teaspoon turmeric
200 ml/¾ cup hot fish stock
400 g/14 oz. can chopped tomatoes
parsley, to serve

PISTACHIO-CRUSTED SALMON
85 g/½ cup unsalted shelled pistachios, chopped
40 g/¾ cup day-old wholewheat spelt breadcrumbs
finely grated zest and juice of 1 unwaxed lemon
½ teaspoon dried chilli/red pepper flakes
4 wild salmon fillets, skin-on
sea salt and cracked black pepper

Low 6 hours, plus 1 hour on high
High 5 hours

Serves 4

Heat the olive oil in a large frying pan/skillet, add the shallots and squash and fry for 5 minutes until slightly softened. Stir in the garlic and fennel seeds and cook for another minute.

Transfer the onion mixture to the slow cooker pot and stir in the artichokes, tomato purée/paste, capers, turmeric, stock and chopped tomatoes. Season with salt and pepper. Cover and cook on low for 6 hours, or high for 4 hours, until the squash is tender.

For the pistachio crust, mix together the pistachios, breadcrumbs, lemon zest and chilli/red pepper flakes in a bowl, then season. Sprinkle the mixture over the top of each salmon fillet, pressing it down to help it stay in place.

Stir the lemon juice into the slow cooker and arrange the salmon fillets on top. Turn the slow cooker to high if on low, and cook for 40–45 minutes until the salmon is opaque. Spoon the vegetable sauce into four large shallow bowls and top each serving with a salmon fillet and a sprinkling of parsley.

NUTRITIONAL INFORMATION
635 kcals, 40 g fat (6.5 g saturates), 23.4 g carbohydrates (12.2 g sugars), 7.5 g fibre, 40 g protein, 1.6 g salt

Seafood tagine with saffron aioli

Don't be put off by the long list of ingredients, this light seafood dish is easy to make, requiring little attention and is the perfect meal for a special occasion.

a pinch of saffron threads

2 tablespoons olive oil

1 large onion, finely chopped

1 red (bell) pepper, deseeded and finely chopped

1 celery stick, finely chopped

3 garlic cloves, finely chopped

2.5-cm/1-in. piece root ginger, (no need to peel), grated

2 teaspoons cumin seeds, ground

2 teaspoons coriander seeds, ground

1½ teaspoons harissa paste, or to taste

400 ml/1¾ cups hot fish stock

coriander/cilantro leaves

1 teaspoon finely grated unwaxed orange zest

juice of 1 large orange

2 tablespoons tomato purée/paste

225 g/8 oz. vine-ripened cherry tomatoes, cut in half

500 g/1 lb. 2 oz. prepared fresh mussels

500 g/1 lb. 2 oz. frozen mixed seafood, such as prawns/shrimp, squid and clams, defrosted and at room temperature, drained well and patted dry

sea salt and cracked black pepper

steamed curly kale, to serve

SAFFRON AIOLI

a pinch saffron threads

1 garlic clove, crushed

1 egg yolk

2 teaspoons Dijon mustard

5 tablespoons cold-pressed rapeseed oil

sea salt and cracked black pepper

Low 6–7 hours, plus 1 hour on high
High 5–6 hours

Serves 4

For the aioli, put the saffron in a ramekin, pour over 1 teaspoon hot water, stir and set aside for 5 minutes. Put the garlic, egg yolk and mustard in a food processor and blend to a thick paste. With the processor running, trickle in the oil to make a sauce the consistency of mayonnaise. Add the saffron and soaking water and season.

Soak the saffron in 2 tablespoons hot water. Heat the olive oil in a large frying pan/skillet, add the onion and fry for 8 minutes until softened. Add the red (bell) pepper, celery, garlic, ginger and ground spices and cook for another minute.

Transfer the vegetable mixture to the slow cooker pot and add the saffron and its soaking liquid, harissa paste, stock, orange zest and juice, tomato purée/paste and tomatoes. Season to taste and stir until mixed together. Cover and cook on low for 6–7 hours, or high for 4–5 hours. If the slow cooker is on low, turn it to high 30 minutes before adding the seafood. Add the mussels and mixed seafood and stir briefly until combined. Cover and cook for a further 25–30 minutes or until heated through and the mussels have opened. Divide the steamed kale between four bowls and spoon the seafood tagine on top. Scatter over the coriander/cilantro serve with the saffron aioli.

NUTRITIONAL INFORMATION
287 kcals, 10.4 g fat (1.7 g saturates), 19.6 g carbohydrate (12.2 g sugars), 4.4 g fibre, 31.4 g protein, 3.4 g salt

Malaysian fish and spinach curry

Cod cheeks are just perfect in curries. The round morsels of white fish are firm enough to keep their shape during cooking, without flaking into nothingness. The spinach adds colour and substance to the curry but is best added towards the end of cooking to retain its fresh green colour, texture and nutrients, including vitamins A, C, E and K, iron, magnesium and folate.

1 large onion, peeled
5-cm/2-in. piece root ginger, roughly chopped
3 garlic cloves, skin removed
1 tablespoon, plus 2 teaspoons coconut oil or ghee
1 tablespoon medium curry powder
3 cardamom pods, seeds ground
2 lemongrass stalks, bruised
1 medium-sized green chilli/chile, deseeded and diced
1 teaspoon turmeric
400 g/14 oz. can coconut milk
100 ml/⅓ cup hot fish stock

400 g/14 oz. sweet potato, peeled and cut into bite-sized pieces
600 g/1 lb. 5 oz. cod cheeks, or thick white fish fillets, cut into 50 g/2 oz. pieces, patted dry
good squeeze of lime juice
75 g/2 packed cups baby spinach leaves, finely chopped
600 g/1 lb. 5 oz. cauliflower florets
sea salt and cracked black pepper

Low 4 hours, plus 25 minutes on high
High 3 hours

Serves 4

Blitz the onion, ginger and garlic in a mini food processor to a coarse paste.

Heat 1 tablespoon coconut oil or ghee in a large frying pan/skillet, add the onion mixture and fry for 5 minutes. Stir in the curry powder, ground cardamom seeds, lemongrass, chilli/chile and turmeric and cook for another minute. Pour in the coconut milk and fish stock and bring almost to the boil, then stir in the sweet potatoes.

Transfer the sweet potato mixture to the slow cooking pot. Cover and cook on low for 4 hours, or high for 2½ hours, until the sweet potato is just tender.

Turn the slow cooker to high if on low. Gently fold in the fish and season with salt and pepper. Replace the lid and cook for 15 minutes. Finally, add the lime juice and spinach, trying not to leave the lid off for too long, and cook for another 5–8 minutes until just tender.

Meanwhile, make the cauliflower rice. Blitz the cauliflower into fine grains in the food processor (or coarsely grate). Heat the remaining 2 teaspoons coconut oil or ghee in a large frying pan/skillet, add the cauliflower and cook, stirring, for 5 minutes until heated through and slightly softened. Serve the 'rice' with the fish curry.

NUTRITIONAL INFORMATION
524 kcals, 25.2 g fat (20.4 g saturates), 34.7 g carbohydrate (15.4 g sugars), 8.1 g fibre, 34.3 g protein, 0.9 g salt

Tandoori-spiced chicken

A great alternative to the traditional roast chicken, the bird is marinated in a coating of spices and cooked slowly until tender and deliciously moist. Serve the chicken with the spiced gravy, or as part of a mixed leaf and radish salad with the Apple Raita on page 36.

3 tablespoons tandoori spice mix
1 tablespoon ground cumin
1 tablespoon ground coriander
3 tablespoons ghee or coconut oil
2 limes, cut in half
1.5 kg/3 lb. 5 oz. free-range chicken
1 onion, cut into 4 slices horizontally
1 tablespoon kuzu or cornflour/cornstarch
sea salt and cracked black pepper
Apple Raita (see page 36), to serve (optional)

Low 7–8 hours
High 4–5 hours

Serves 4

NUTRITIONAL
INFORMATION
622 kcals, 44 g fat (17.2 g saturates), 6.7 g carbohydrate (2.6 g sugars), 2.3 g fibre, 48 g protein, 0.5 g salt

Mix together all the spices with half the ghee or coconut oil. Add the juice of 1 lime and season with salt and pepper. Put the chicken in a shallow dish and, with gloved hands, rub the spice mixture all over the chicken until evenly coated. Place the dish in a plastic bag, seal, and leave the chicken to marinate in the fridge for at least 4 hours or overnight, if time allows.

Take the chicken out of the fridge 1 hour before you plan to cook it. Remove and discard the plastic bag. Heat the remaining 2 tablespoons ghee or coconut oil in a large sauté pan/skillet over a medium-high heat and brown the chicken all over until golden, using tongs to help you turn the bird – this will take about 10–15 minutes.

Put the onion slices in the base of the slow cooker pot and place the chicken on top. Put the remaining lime halves inside the cavity of the bird and pour over any cooking juices. Cover and cook on low for 7–8 hours, or high for 4–5 hours, until the chicken is cooked through, the juices run clear and there is no trace of pink when the thickest part of the thigh is pierced with a small knife. Carefully remove the chicken from the pot and cover it loosely with foil to keep warm.

The chicken will produce a handsome amount of spicy juices, which make a great base for gravy. Scoop off any fat on the surface, then mash the onion into the juices. Mix the kuzo or cornflour/cornstarch with a little cold water and stir into the slow cooker pot. Cook, uncovered, on a high heat for another 10 minutes until thickened, stirring regularly. Alternatively, pour the gravy into a small pan, add the kuzo or cornflour/cornstarch mixture and simmer, stirring, over a medium heat until thickened. Carve the chicken and serve with the spiced gravy.

Chicken mole with raw cacao

Richly spiced and enlivened with smoky chipotle chilli/chile, raw cacao powder and peanut butter, this classic Mexican stew is perfect served with the traditional accompaniments of corn tortillas and guacamole – I also like it with the fresh, crisp Pickled Red Cabbage.

2 red onions, diced

3 garlic cloves, finely chopped

1 medium-sized green chilli/chile, deseeded and finely chopped

1 tablespoon chipotle chilli/chile paste, or 1 tablespoon hot smoked paprika

2 teaspoons ground coriander

2 teaspoons ground cumin

½ cinnamon stick

400 g/14 oz. can chopped tomatoes

25 g/1 oz. dried pitted dates, diced

2 tablespoons peanut butter

6 skinless chicken thighs on the bone

100 ml/⅓ cup hot chicken stock

2 teaspoons raw cacao powder or cocoa powder

sea salt and cracked black pepper

PICKLED RED CABBAGE

100 g/3½ oz. red cabbage, shredded

1 large carrot, coarsely grated

2 tablespoons apple cider vinegar

1 teaspoon maple syrup

½ teaspoons fennel seeds

TO SERVE

flatbreads or brown rice

sliced avocado, chopped coriander/ cilantro

Low 7–8 hours
High 4–5 hours

Serves 4

Mix together the red onions, garlic, chilli/chile, chipotle paste or paprika, spices, chopped tomatoes, dates and peanut butter in a large bowl. Add the chicken and spoon the onion mixture over to coat the thighs all over. Leave the chicken to marinate for 1 hour or so, or overnight, covered, in the fridge.

When ready to cook, tip the chicken and its marinade into the slow cooker pot. Pour in the hot stock. Cover and cook on low for 7–8 hours, or high for 4–5 hours, until the chicken is cooked through.

To make the pickled red cabbage, mix together all the ingredients in a bowl and season with salt and pepper.

Lift the thighs out of the sauce onto a plate and, using two forks, pull the chicken away from the bones in strips. Discard the bones.

Stir the cacao or cocoa powder and shredded chicken into the sauce. Season to taste. Serve the mole on flatbreads or rice, topped with slices of avocado, chopped coriander/cilantro and a spoonful of the pickled red cabbage.

NUTRITIONAL INFORMATION
376 kcals, 14.2 g fat (4.1 g saturates), 16.4 g carbohydrate (13.1 g sugars), 4.1 g fibre, 44 g protein, 1 g salt

Chicken dhansak

Spices feature prominently in my cooking as does garlic, as you can see from this protein-rich chicken and lentil curry. High status in superfood terms, garlic has numerous impressive health properties and has been linked to a reduced risk of heart disease, lowered levels of harmful blood cholesterol and improved circulation.

2 onions, roughly chopped

4-cm/1½-in. piece root ginger, roughly chopped

6 garlic cloves, peeled

1 medium-sized red chilli/chile, deseeded and cut in half

2 teaspoons coriander seeds

1 teaspoon cumin seeds

2 teaspoons panch phoran

1 tablespoon ghee or coconut oil

½ cinnamon stick

1 teaspoon turmeric

½ teaspoon chilli/red pepper flakes

125 g/⅔ cup split red lentils, rinsed

500 ml/2 cups hot chicken stock

2 tablespoons tomato purée/paste

3 tomatoes, deseeded and diced

280 g/10 oz. butternut squash, peeled, deseeded and diced

1 tablespoon tamarind paste or lemon juice

6 skinless chicken thighs on the bone

sea salt and cracked black pepper

brown basmati rice and coriander/cilantro leaves, to serve

Low 7–8 hours
High 4–5 hours

Serves 4

Put the onions, ginger, garlic and chilli/chili in a food processor and blitz to a coarse paste. Grind the coriander seeds, cumin seeds and panch phoran in a pestle and mortar.

Heat the ghee or coconut oil in a large frying pan/skillet, add the onion mixture and fry for 5 minutes, then stir in the ground spices.

Tip the onion mixture into the slow cooker pot and add the cinnamon stick, turmeric, chilli/red pepper flakes, lentils, stock, tomato purée/paste, tomatoes, squash and tamarind paste or lemon juice. Stir well until combined, then press the chicken thighs into the lentil mixture.

Cover and cook on low for 7–8 hours, or high for 4–5 hours, until the lentils are tender and the chicken is cooked through. Lift the thighs out of the sauce onto a plate and, using two forks, pull the chicken away from the bones in chunks. Discard the bones and pick out the cinnamon stick from the lentil sauce. Return the chicken to the pot, adding more hot stock or water, if needed.

Taste the dhansak and add more chilli/red pepper flakes, if needed, and season with salt and pepper. Serve the dhansak with rice, scattered with coriander/cilantro.

NUTRITIONAL INFORMATION
446 kcals, 11.2 g fat (4.6 g saturates), 34.7 g carbohydrate (14.4 g sugars), 6.9 g fibre, 48 g protein, 1.6 g salt

Duck with nectarines

It's not always necessary to brown meat and poultry before slow cooking, but here it helps to add colour to the duck as well as drain off some of the fat found in the skin. Chinese spices, ginger and fruit are classic partners with duck, particularly as they help to cut through the richness of the meat. Try to use nectarines that are ripe, but not overly, so they hold their shape during cooking.

4 large duck legs, trimmed of any excess skin
2 teaspoons Chinese five spice
1½ teaspoons ground ginger
2.5 cm/1 in. piece root ginger, sliced
2 teaspoons reduced-salt soy sauce
70 g/½ cup frozen shelled edamame beans, defrosted
2–3 just-ripe nectarines (depending on size) stone/pit removed and sliced
1 tablespoon kuzu or cornflour/cornstarch
sea salt and cracked black pepper
brown basmati rice, coriander/cilantro and steamed long-stem broccoli, to serve

Low 7–8 hours
High 4–5 hours

Serves 4

Season the duck legs with salt and pepper. Place two of the legs, skin-side down, in an unheated large sauté pan/skillet on a medium-high heat and cook until the skin is golden and starting to crisp. Turn the duck over and brown the other side of the legs – this takes about 10 minutes in total. Transfer the browned duck legs to a plate, pour off any fat in the sauté pan/skillet and repeat with the remaining two duck legs.

Mix together the five spice, ground ginger, root ginger, soy sauce and 100 ml/⅓ cup hot water in the slow cooker pot. Place the browned duck legs on top. Cover and cook on low for 6 hours, or high for 3 hours. Tuck the edamame and nectarines around the duck, so they are submerged in the sauce, cover, and cook for another 1 hour.

Mix the kuzu or cornflour with a little water and set aside. Using a slotted spoon, remove the duck legs, root ginger, nectarines and edamame from the pot. Discard the ginger.

Scoop off any fat on the surface of the sauce. Stir the kuzu or cornflour/cornstarch mixture into the sauce with another 150 ml/⅔ cup hot water. Turn the slow cooker to high if on low, cover and cook for 10 minutes until the sauce has thickened to a smooth gravy-like consistency. Stir well.

Return the duck, nectarines and edamame to the slow cooker to warm through. Serve with the sauce, rice, coriander/cilantro and steamed long-stem broccoli.

NUTRITIONAL INFORMATION
461 kcals, 30.2 g fat (8.7 g saturates), 9.7 g carbohydrate (5.5 g sugars), 2.3 g fibre, 36.5 g protein, 2 g salt

Venison, chestnut and apple casserole

Venison has more protein than any other meat and is an excellent source of many B vitamins, zinc as well as energy-giving iron. It is a lean meat, so there is very little wastage, and when slow cooked becomes beautifully tender. Here, it's combined with shallots, carrots, parsnips, apple and chestnuts to make a heart-warming, comforting meal that's full of goodness.

1 rounded tablespoon spelt flour

500 g/1 lb. 2 oz. lean stewing venison or beef

1 tablespoon olive oil

300 g/10½ oz. shallots, cut in half (leave the root ends intact)

2 carrots, chopped

2 parsnips, chopped

1 celery stick, thinly sliced

2 large garlic cloves, finely chopped

175 g/6 oz. cooked peeled chestnuts, cut in half

2 teaspoons finely chopped fresh rosemary

1 tablespoon juniper berries, crushed

1 apple, cored and cut into bite-sized chunks

600 ml/2½ cups hot beef stock

sea salt and cracked black pepper

Low 7–8 hours
High 5–6 hours

Serves 4

Put the flour on a plate and season it with salt and pepper. Add the venison or beef and turn to lightly coat the meat in the seasoned flour.

Heat the oil in a large deep sauté pan/skillet over a medium-high heat, add the meat and cook until browned all over – this takes about 10 minutes. Stir in the shallots, carrots, parsnips, celery, garlic, chestnuts, rosemary and juniper and cook for another 5 minutes.

Transfer the venison or beef mixture to the slow cooker, adding a splash of water to the pan/skillet to help release any brown bits stuck to the bottom and pour these into the slow cooker. Add half the apple and stock and stir until combined. Cover and cook on low for 7–8 hours, or high for 5–6 hours, until the venison or beef is tender. Add the remaining apple 2 hours before the end of the cooking time so it retains its shape and texture.

Check the seasoning at the end of the cooking time and add more, if needed. Serve the stew with some green vegetables and your favourite mash – carrot, sweet potato, parsnip, celeriac, swede/rutabaga or butternut squash are all good alternatives to the more usual potato.

NUTRITIONAL INFORMATION
410 kcals, 10.3 g fat (2.7 g saturates), 39.6 g carbohydrate (19.3 g sugars), 12.3 g fibre, 33.6 g protein, 1.4 g salt

Bone broth pho

A labour of love, this gut-healing Vietnamese pho (pronounced 'fuh') is made with the 12-hour Bone Broth on page 16, but if making your own stock is a step too far or time is against you, do opt for a good-quality, ready-made fresh beef stock instead. The use of wholewheat noodles is a break from tradition as rice noodles are the norm but they offer little in the way of nutrients, although they are gluten free – the beauty of pho is that you can adapt it to suit your own tastes.

1 litre/4 cups hot 12-hour Bone Broth (see page 16), or good-quality fresh beef stock

1 onion, thinly sliced

3 star anise

5-cm/2-in. piece root ginger, sliced into thin rounds

2 lemongrass stalks, bruised

4 garlic cloves, thinly sliced

1 medium-sized red chilli/chile, split lengthways

1 tablespoon fish sauce

1 tablespoon reduced-salt soy sauce

2 pak choi/bok choy, cut in half lengthways

240 g/8½ oz. wholewheat noodles

1 teaspoon cold-pressed rapeseed oil

2 x 200 g/7 oz. sirloin/porterhouse beef steaks, patted dry

TO SERVE
beansprouts, spring onions/scallions, thinly sliced diagonally, mint, basil, red chilli/chile, deseeded and cut into thin strips

Low 4–5 hours
High 3–4 hours

Serves 4

Put the hot bone broth, onion, star anise, ginger, lemongrass, garlic and whole chilli/chile in the slow cooker pot. Cover and cook on low for 4–5 hours, or high for 3–4 hours, to let the flavourings infuse the broth.

Using a slotted spoon, scoop out and discard the flavourings and add the fish sauce, soy sauce and pak choi/bok choy to the broth. Turn the slow cooker to high if on low, cover and cook for 20–30 minutes until the pak choi/bok choy is just tender.

While the pak choi/bok choy is cooking, cook the noodles in a separate pan according to the packet instructions, then drain and set aside.

Heat a large, heavy-based frying pan/skillet over a high heat. Turn the heat to medium-high, add the oil and heat through. Season the steaks and sear for about 2 minutes on each side, or until cooked the way you like them. Remove the steaks from the pan, cover with foil to keep warm and leave to rest while you assemble the pho.

Divide the cooked noodles between four large shallow bowls and ladle over the broth, allowing one half of pak choi/bok choy per serving. Slice the beef thinly on the diagonal and arrange on top, pouring over juices left on the plate. Serve with the garnishes by the side.

NUTRITIONAL INFORMATION
414 kcals, 5.9 g fat (2.3 g saturates), 55 g carbohydrate (9.1 g sugars), 7.1 g fibre, 31.8 g protein, 4.1 g salt

Pulled pork lettuce cups

To lend a healthy twist to this recipe, the pulled pork is shredded and served in a Little Gem lettuce leaf with quinoa and topped with a crisp zingy pickle.

Heat the oil in a large, deep sauté pan/skillet over a medium-high heat and sear the pork until browned all over – this will take about 10–15 minutes. Transfer the pork to a plate.

Mix together the smoked paprika, mustard powder, ginger, tomato purée/paste, vinegar and maple syrup. Season with salt and pepper, then spread three-quarters of the rub all over the pork. You could leave the pork to marinate for 1 hour, if time allows.

Place the onion and carrot in an even layer in the bottom of the slow cooker pot, pour in 2 tablespoons water and top with the pork. Cover and cook on low for 8–10 hours until the pork is tender and almost falling apart, but not quite. Carefully lift the pork out of the pot onto a plate, cover with foil and leave to rest while you finish cooking the sauce.

Strain the juices in the pot into a small saucepan, pressing the onion and carrot through the sieve/strainer. Stir in the remaining rub and cook until reduced and thickened.

Shred the pork into strips, discarding any fat. Put the pork on a large serving plate and spoon enough of the sauce over to lightly coat the meat.

To serve, arrange the Little Gem leaves on a serving plate and the quinoa, coriander/cilantro and pickle in separate serving bowls. Let everyone help themselves, placing a spoonful of the quinoa in a lettuce leaf and topping it with some of the pulled pork, a spoonful of pickle and a sprinkling of sesame seeds and coriander/cilantro.

1 tablespoon cold-pressed rapeseed oil
1 tablespoon hot smoked paprika
1 tablespoon English mustard powder
1 teaspoon ground ginger
2 heaped tablespoons tomato purée/paste
1 tablespoon apple cider vinegar
2 tablespoons maple syrup
1.5 kg/3 lb. 5 oz. skinless, boneless pork shoulder/ Boston butt, excess fat trimmed, tied with twine
1 large onion, cut into 8 thin wedges
1 large carrot, thickly sliced
sea salt and black pepper

TO SERVE
Little Gem leaves, cooked quinoa, 3 x quantity Pickled Red Cabbage (see page 127), toasted sesame seeds, chopped coriander/cilantro leaves

Low 8–10 hours

Serves 10–12

NUTRITIONAL INFORMATION
247 kcals, 9.3 g fat (2.3 g saturates), 8 g carbohydrate (5.5 g sugars), 32.2 g protein, 0.4 g salt

Winter beef and prune pot roast

No bells and whistles... just sustaining, hearty, feel-good food that's cooked simply. For the best flavour, buy good-quality grass-fed organic beef and ensure the joint is an even cylindrical shape and not tapered at the ends so it cooks evenly without drying out. The prunes/dried plums lend a touch of sweetness as well as a healthy dose of fibre and minerals.

1 kg/2 lb. 4 oz. grass-reared silverside or topside beef joint/top round/ bottom round, any external fat removed, tied with twine
2 tablespoons olive oil
3 carrots, quartered lengthways and sliced
1 large onion, halved and thinly sliced
1 celery stick, thinly sliced
2 turnips, cut into small bite-sized pieces
3 bay leaves
4 long thyme sprigs or 1 teaspoon dried thyme
3 garlic cloves, crushed
500 ml/2 cups hot 12-hour Bone Broth (see page 12) or good-quality fresh beef stock
100 g/½ cup dried pitted prunes/dried plums
1 rounded tablespoon kuzu or cornflour/cornstarch
15 g/1 tablespoon butter or ghee
sea salt cracked black pepper

Low 7–9 hours
High 5–6 hours

Serves 6

Season the beef with salt and pepper. Heat half the oil in a large deep sauté pan/skillet and sear the beef, turning it occasionally, until browned all over – this will take about 10 minutes.

Remove the beef from the pan/skillet, add the remaining oil and sauté the carrots, onion, celery and turnips for 5 minutes until starting to soften. Add the bay leaves, thyme, garlic and stock and stir to loosen any bits that have stuck to the base of the pan. Place the vegetable mixture in the slow cooker pot.

Add the beef and prunes/dried plums to the pot and spoon over the gravy. Cover and cook on low for 7–9 hours, or high for 5–6 hours, until the beef is tender. Turn the beef over halfway through the cooking time to prevent the top drying out.

Using a slotted spoon, remove the beef, vegetables and prunes/dried plums to a dish and cover with foil to keep warm.

To thicken the gravy, mix the kuzu or cornflour/cornstarch with a little cold water and stir it into the slow cooker pot. Cook, uncovered, on the high setting for another 10 minutes until thickened, stirring regularly. Alternatively, pour the juices into a small pan. Add the kuzu or cornflour/cornstarch mixture and simmer, stirring, over a medium heat until thickened. Finally, stir the butter or ghee into the gravy until melted.

Snip off the twine around the beef and carve into slices. Serve the beef with the prunes/dried plums, vegetables and gravy.

NUTRITIONAL INFORMATION
434 kcals, 17.9 g fat (5.6 g saturates), 19.9 g carbohydrate (16.3 g sugars), 5.1 g fibre, 44.7 g protein, 0.7 g salt

Piri piri lamb salad

Chillies/chiles contain impressive health benefits from supporting immunity and heart health to pain reduction and weight loss.

½ small red (bell) pepper, deseeded and chopped

2 medium-sized red chillies/chiles

2 smoked garlic cloves, or regular garlic cloves, skin removed

1 tablespoon apple cider vinegar

5 tablespoons extra virgin olive oil, plus extra for browning

1 tablespoon hot smoked paprika

2 teaspoons dried oregano

1 teaspoon maple syrup

1 kg/2 lb. 4 oz. lamb half shoulder on the bone/shoulder roast, excess fat trimmed

1 large onion, cut into wedges

1 carrot, sliced

sea salt and cracked black pepper

flatbreads, to serve

CAULIFLOWER TABBOULEH

1 small cauliflower, separated into florets

6 tomatoes, diced

½ cucumber, diced

1 small red onion, diced

8 radishes, sliced into rounds

2 tablespoons extra virgin olive oil

finely grated zest and juice of 1 unwaxed lemon

2 handfuls freshly chopped parsley

2 handfuls freshly chopped mint

sea salt and cracked black pepper

3 tablespoons toasted flaked almonds, to serve

Low 9–10 hours

Serves 6

To make the piri piri sauce, put the red (bell) pepper, chillies/chiles, garlic, vinegar and olive oil in a mini food processor and blend to a purée. Stir in the paprika, oregano and maple syrup and season.

Heat a splash of olive oil in a large, deep sauté pan/skillet over a medium-high heat and sear the lamb until browned all over – this takes about 10 minutes. Transfer the lamb to a plate. Spoon over about half of the piri piri sauce until the lamb is coated all over. Reserve the remaining sauce. Put the onion and carrot in the base of the slow cooker pot and top with the lamb, adding any juices left in the pan. Cover and cook on low for 9–10 hours until the lamb is soft and starting to fall off the bone.

For the tabbouleh, blitz the cauliflower into small grain-sized pieces in a food processor. Tip into a large shallow serving bowl and add the tomatoes, cucumber, onion and radishes. Mix together the olive oil, lemon zest and juice and season with salt and pepper. Pour the dressing mixture over the tabbouleh, add the herbs and gently stir until combined. Scatter over the almonds just before serving so they keep their crunchy texture.

Remove the lamb from the slow cooker and pull the meat off the bone in thick strips. Place on a plate and cover with foil to keep warm.

Strain the juices from the pot into a bowl and scoop off any fat on the surface. Press the onion and carrot through the sieve/strainer into the meat juices to make a gravy. Spoon some of the gravy over the lamb. Serve the lamb with the tabbouleh, flatbreads and the remaining piri piri sauce.

NUTRITIONAL INFORMATION
456 kcals, 36.5 g fat (13.1 g saturates),
6.1 g carbohydrate (5 g sugars),
2.3 g fibre, 24.4 g protein, 0.3 g salt

Index

Acknowledgments

This book has been a joy to write and work on, and much of that is
due to the great team at RPS. A big, heartfelt thanks goes to Julia Charles
for commissioning me and her support and enthusiasm over the years
that we have worked together. Thank you, too, to Cathy Seward for her
experienced, practical and supportive advice on all matters slow-cooker—
it was also great to have your help double testing the recipes. I'm beyond
happy with the beautiful photographs by Peter Cassidy, the food styling
by Kathy Kordalis and Sian Henley, prop styling by Luis Peral and design
by Sonya Nathoo – you all made my recipes look so good. I would also
like to thank Miriam Catley for her editing skills and calm efficiency.
Nicola Graimes

This has been a hugely enjoyable book to work on with Nicola and the
whole team at Ryland Peters and Small. Thank you to everyone.
Cathy Seward